Ancient Miamians

NATIVE PEOPLES, CULTURES, AND PLACES OF THE SOUTHEASTERN UNITED STATES

Florida A&M University, Tallahassee
Florida Atlantic University, Boca Raton
Florida Gulf Coast University, Ft. Myers
Florida International University, Miami
Florida State University, Tallahassee
University of Central Florida, Orlando
University of Florida, Gainesville
University of North Florida, Jacksonville
University of South Florida, Tampa
University of West Florida, Pensacola

Native Peoples, Cultures, and Places of the Southeastern United States
EDITED BY JERALD T. MILANICH

The Apalachee Indians and Mission San Luis,
by John H. Hann and Bonnie G. McEwan (1998)
Florida's Indians from Ancient Times to the Present, by Jerald T. Milanich (1998)
Unconquered People: Florida's Seminole and Miccosukee Indians,
by Brent R. Weisman (1999)
The Ancient Mounds of Poverty Point: Place of Rings, by Jon L. Gibson (2000)
Before and After Jamestown: Virginia's Powhatans and Their Predecessors,
by Helen C. Rountree and E. Randolph Turner III (2002)
Ancient Miamians: The Tequesta of South Florida, by William E. McGoun (2002)

Ancient Miamians

The Tequesta of South Florida

William E. McGoun

University Press of Florida

GAINESVILLE · TALLAHASSEE · TAMPA · BOCA RATON
PENSACOLA · ORLANDO · MIAMI · JACKSONVILLE · FT. MYERS

07 06 05 04 03 02   6 5 4 3 2 1

LIBRARY OF CONGRESS CATALOGING-IN-PUBLICATION DATA
McGoun, William E., 1937–
Ancient Miamians: the Tequesta of South Florida / William E. McGoun
p. cm. — (Native peoples, cultures, and places
of the southeastern United States)
Includes bibliographical references and index.
ISBN 0-8130-2495-1 (cloth: alk. paper)
1. Tequesta Indians. I. Title. II. Series.
E99.T325 M34 2002
975.9'3—dc21 2001054015

The University Press of Florida is the scholarly publishing agency for
the State University System of Florida, comprising Florida A&M Uni-
versity, Florida Atlantic University, Florida Gulf Coast University, Florida International University, Florida State University, University of
Central Florida, University of Florida, University of North Florida,
University of South Florida, and University of West Florida.

University Press of Florida
15 Northwest 15th Street
Gainesville, FL 32611–2079
http://www.upf.com

Contents

Foreword

Driving across the MacArthur Causeway from Miami to Miami Beach, most residents of and visitors to Florida's Gold Coast are not aware they are duplicating a journey made thousands of times in the past by American Indians. Five centuries ago Miami and Key Biscayne were the realm of the Tequesta Indians, a people whose ancestors had lived in the region for thousands of years. They plied the waters of Biscayne Bay in dugout canoes, traveling back and forth among their villages and fishing and shellfish-gathering camps.

Where today there are hotels and other buildings at the mouth of the Miami River, there was a major Tequesta Indian village. When late-nineteenth-century settlers and entrepreneurs founded Miami, shell and earth middens left behind by the Tequesta and their ancestors blanketed both banks of the Miami River near Brickell Point. Sand mounds and one mound of stone could be seen, sites where the Indians once buried their dead. The Miami Circle, which received so much attention in the late 1990s, lies within that Brickell Point site. Before Miami was Miami, it was Indian territory.

Indeed, the name Miami comes from a South Florida Indian name for Lake Okeechobee.

In this popularly written book, archaeologist and journalist William McGoun brings us the story of the Indians who lived in the Miami area. Drawing on the latest information excavated from Dade County sites by archaeologists such as Robert S. Carr, who has worked in the areas for several decades, McGoun paints a vivid picture of the Tequesta and the people who preceded them. He enlivens their history by using archaeologically derived information to put together vignettes about native people like those who once lived in the region, giving voice and action to the past.

This well-illustrated account is a welcome addition to our series about the Native Peoples, Cultures, and Places of the Southeastern United States.

Jerald T. Milanich
Series Editor

Preface

Reconstructing the everyday and not-so-everyday routines of people who lived hundreds or thousands of years ago is a difficult task. Consider how often some revelation in the news reminds us how little we know about those among whom we live today, despite a wealth, perhaps a superabundance, of written information. For the Ancient Miamians we have no writing at all aside from a very few Spanish accounts, and these only from the final two centuries of a tradition that endured for 10,000 years.

The device I have employed is the "a day in the life" approach used so effectively by Oscar Lewis in illuminating the life of contemporary Mexicans. The days I have chosen occurred in 8,000 B.C., 2,000 B.C., 500 B.C., A.D. 500, A.D. 1568, A.D. 1761, and today. With the exception of the last day, I have been at a disadvantage in that I could not interview the people about whom I wrote but rather had to depend on the archaeological and historical record.

The dates were selected because, first, they fall within significant stages in the development of what most archaeologists call the Glades cultural area and, second, there is archaeological evidence for each date from at least one site in Miami-Dade County. The earliest date is squarely within what is called the Paleoindian Period, the time of the first human occupation of South Florida. The second falls within the Archaic Period, when the paleoindian big-game hunters were replaced by people who essentially ate whatever they could find or catch. The rest represent various stages in what is called the Glades periods, which began with the first appearance of pottery tempered with sand and ended when the aboriginal cultures became extinct in the eighteenth century.

Little archaeological work was done in Miami-Dade County until well into the twentieth century, and even less is readily available. For instance, John M. Goggin, the first chair of anthropology at the

CULTURAL PERIODS IN PREHISTORIC SOUTH FLORIDA

Period	Dates	Characteristics
Paleoindian	10,000–7000 B.C.	Distinctive lithic artifacts; evidence of human presence in association with remains of extinct Pleistocene animals
Early Archaic	7000–5000 B.C.	Stemmed projectile points
Middle Archaic	5000–3000 B.C.	Sites in southeast Florida
Late Archaic	3000–1500 B.C.	More sites, notably in southeast Florida
Transitional	1500–500 B.C.	Appearance of fiber-tempered pottery
Glades I	500 B.C.–A.D. 800	Sand-tempered pottery; rim incising
Glades II	A.D. 800–1200	Incising of rims dies out on Gulf Coast, persists on East Coast
Glades III	A.D. 1200–1566	Incising decreases; rim-tooling appears; check-stamping appears
Historic	A.D. 1566–1763	European objects

The Hyatt Hotel towers over the Granada site, where
Tequesta Indians lived. Photo by Bonnie McGoun.

University of Florida, listed information on more than fifty sites in
a manuscript prepared in 1949 for Yale University Publications in
Anthropology but never published. Only a small number of copies
were printed of the most extensive report ever on a single location
in Miami-Dade, the two-volume work on the Granada site, home of
the historic Tequesta Indians, prepared by the Florida Division of
Archives, History and Records Management for the City of Miami.
In the first volume John W. Griffin and eight coauthors cover the
archaeological record. In the second, Arva Moore Parks reviews the
historical record.

Surfside mounds as they looked in 1927 after land had been cleared for development. Courtesy Florida State Archives.

General discussions that touch on Miami-Dade appear in many works. There are brief mentions in Charlton W. Tebeau's *A History of Florida*, Jerald T. Milanich's *Archaeology of Precolumbian Florida*, and in chapters by Milanich, Eugene Lyon, and John H. Hann in Michael Gannon's *New History of Florida*. The most detail in any previously published work is in my *Prehistoric Peoples of South Florida*, and that isn't much.

The Surfside mounds, the setting for chapter 3 of this book, are discussed in some detail in John Kunkel Small's *From Eden to Sahara: Florida's Tragedy*. Generally, however, detailed archaeological accounts are available in published form only in articles in *Florida Anthropologist* magazine.

Any attempt to go beyond a recitation of pottery and point styles, to get to the people behind the objects, by necessity involves a lot of assumptions. Some of these assumptions, such as the ways those objects were made, have a solid foundation in fact. Others, especially when they involve beliefs, are by necessity speculative. This book frequently relies on analogies from other times and other places to fill in the record. Some of these assumptions may be broadly shared; others may be unique or nearly so. As one example, few share my acceptance of William H. Sears's assumption that the Green Corn Ceremony is at least 2,000 years old.

This work is not footnoted in the standard academic manner. The casual reader is not interested in researching original sources and finds notes to be nuisances that interrupt a train of thought. Nevertheless, there are bibliographic essays for each chapter and a full list of references at the end of the book. For those wanting more detail, almost every book or periodical cited in the reference section is available in the Miami-Dade County Public Library.

This book could not have been possible without Jerald T. Milanich. Besides being general editor of this series and the source of a lot of advice, he was my adviser during my doctoral program and encouraged me to use my writing skills, such as they are, to prepare accounts of prehistoric people that would be accessible to the general public.

Robert S. Carr of the Archaeological and Historical Conservancy and the staff of the Miami-Dade Historic Preservation Division provided invaluable help with both information and illustrations. Finally, and by no means least, are the contributions of my wife, Bonnie, who took some of the pictures for this volume and put up with me closeting myself in my den to write it.

Introduction

The Beginning of the End

The first date on which Miami appears in the historical record is May 13, 1513, but that day is more important to us today than it was to anyone then. To the Spanish visitors, it was just another day in their slow trip down the east coast of Florida. To the Indians of the region, it was just another day, period.

The Spaniards' three ships, under the command of Juan Ponce de León, remained close to shore to stay out of the northward-flowing Gulf Stream current. When Ponce saw something interesting inside one of the inlets, he would dispatch sailors in a ship's boat to explore while the rest of the company remained on shipboard in deeper water offshore. On May 13, according to the account of Antonio de Herrera as analyzed by T. Frederick Davis in *Florida Historical Quarterly,* the object was a large bay near the southern end of Florida. It must have been the one that later would be named El Biscaino, for his home on the Bay of Biscay, by a Spanish sailor who

1

Juan Ponce de León (*inset*) and battle near Fort Myers (*left*), in seventeenth-century engraving.

was shipwrecked and married into the Tequesta Indians before being rescued.

If they penetrated far enough, the explorers hardly could have missed an Indian village on the north shore of the Miami River, where today's Ramada DuPont Plaza and Hyatt hotels stand. But that is probably all they found. For one thing, food shortages in spring and summer would force the aborigines to scatter in search of nuts, berries, turtles, and fish. For another, if the people had noticed the ships, they had very good reasons not to make their presence known.

History books say Ponce "discovered" Florida on April 2 when the ships reached land somewhere between St. Augustine and Cape Canaveral. But a peninsula that looks a lot like Florida appears on the Cantino map of 1502, and that map may have been copied from earlier sources. A body of water that could be Lake Okeechobee shows up on Juan de la Cosa's 1500 map, the first known depiction of the New World on a world map. Both maps are reproduced by Peter Whitfield in his book *The Charting of the Oceans*.

Those earlier visitors had a single purpose: to capture Indians to work the mines of Hispaniola. Christopher Columbus had sought royal permission to enslave Indians as early as 1494, and by the time of Ponce both the Greater Antilles and the Bahamas had been largely depopulated. The Florida raids hardly would have endeared the Spanish to the Indians, which goes a long way toward explaining their hostility to Ponce. The Indians didn't have to read the written authorization for Ponce's voyage, in which he was empowered to "allot" the Indians among his party. They knew what likely was in store.

Everywhere Ponce landed, the Indians pulled in the welcome mat. The first encounter occurred somewhere between Cape Canaveral and Palm Beach, possibly near the mouth of the Loxahatchee River at Jupiter, on April 20, 1513, when Ponce went ashore and called out to the Indians. They answered by trying to seize the Spaniards' boat, oars, and weapons. One Spaniard was knocked cold with a club, and two others were wounded with arrows or spears.

On June 4, near Fort Myers, on the west coast of the peninsula, the Spaniards were lured by an Indian who spoke Spanish into waiting for the Indian leader to visit—another pretty good indication of previous contact. Instead, the Spaniards were assailed by a canoe-borne raiding party that killed one Spaniard before being driven off. Two days later there was another battle. Ponce never did get to meet the leader, whom he called Carlos.

Early in July, Ponce sailed past Miami again. The written records make no mention of a landing there, though it would be two more weeks before Ponce reached the Bahamas, suggesting he spent some time ashore somewhere. Herrera refers to Chequescha, certainly a

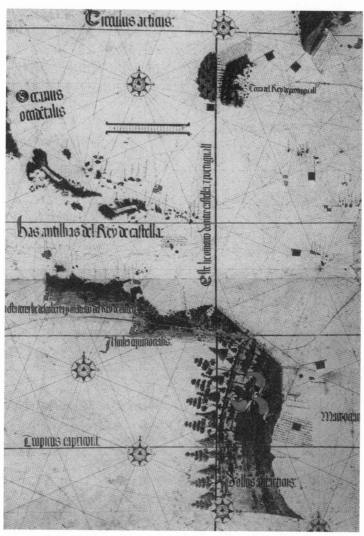

What appears to be Florida at upper right of Cantino map,
which dates from 1502.

variant of Tequesta, the name the Spanish used later for both the village and the people who lived at the mouth of the Miami River. The map drafted in 1514–15 by Comte Ottomanno Freducci, analyzed by Jerald T. Milanich and Nara B. Milanich in another *Florida Historical Quarterly* article, shows a Chequiche, obviously another variant of Tequesta.

The fact that Herrera mentions the name Chequescha at this point in his narrative suggests that Ponce first met some of the inhabitants on the July journey. He probably already knew of their existence from earlier Spanish visitors, from Indians he had met during his trip, or even through earlier, unreported visits of his own.

What he could not have known is that the Tequesta were not the first Miamians, not by a long shot. Today's Miami-Dade County had been inhabited for 10,000 years, longer than sixteenth-century Europeans believed the earth had existed. These earlier Florida Indians had successfully adapted to changes in climate and sea level and wildlife. What they could not adjust to were newcomers with weapons more powerful than any they had ever seen and diseases for which they had no immunity. Within 250 years of Ponce's first Florida voyage, the Indian societies that gave him such a rude welcome would be extinct. What follows is the story of the people who made this land their home for ten millennia, beginning with the little evidence that remains today.

1

In Search of
the Ancient Miamians

"See those two dead trees. It's just about there."

The speaker was Sergeant Frank Reed, a security guard at the Deering Estate on Old Cutler Road in southern Miami-Dade County, and he was pointing out the sinkhole where the county's first visitors found water 10,000 years ago. Florida was much more arid then, and the sea level was more than 300 feet lower. Today the sinkhole sits only a couple of football fields from Biscayne Bay, but 10 millennia ago it was probably at least 10 miles from the nearest water.

Archaeologists call it the Cutler Fossil site after the bones found there, many from animals that became extinct either before or shortly after the first Miamians arrived. While it contains the oldest evidence of human presence in the county, it was not rediscovered until two collectors removed fossil bones and teeth in 1979. Professional excavation was not undertaken until 1985, after a "pot-hunter" had dug two deep holes and removed hundreds of fossil bones. Pot-hunters are the bane of every archaeologist. In looting a site for souvenirs, they take the items out of context, and context is everything for the professional archaeologist.

When a certain type of pot, or a certain style of arrowhead, is known to be of a particular age, that tells the archaeologist little more than when the site was occupied. The knowledge that takes us beyond dates to understand how ancient people hunted and gathered, how they built shelters and made tools and weapons, how they contended with this world and what they believed about other worlds—that knowledge comes only from studying the relative position of not just pretty pots and arrowheads but such mundane things as a stain in the earth that shows where a wooden post once stood.

The pot-hunter frequently obliterates such subtle evidence as posthole stains and scatters other evidence to and fro in his search

Looking toward the Cutler Fossil site from the visitor center of the Deering Estate. Photo by Bonnie McGoun.

for something pretty or valuable. In southwest Florida, which has produced more gold and silver items made by Indians than has southeast Florida—though even there the amounts have been small—pot-hunters have used bulldozers on Indian mounds, destroying who knows what in a futile search for precious metals.

Fortunately, the Cutler Fossil pot-hunter was caught within a week, and the site was not seriously harmed. Before more damage could be done, the site was excavated by professionals under the direction of Robert S. Carr, then county archaeologist. The pros found wonderful things, not as spectacular as what Howard Carter gazed upon when he first opened King Tut's tomb in 1922 but in their own way just as significant. These things showed that humans had visited Miami-Dade County 6,000 years earlier than previously known. There was a spear point 100 centuries in age and enough bits and pieces of chert to show that the first visitors had made spear points and drills and scrapers there. The points would fell animals, and the drills and scrapers were important in preparing the skins for clothing and shelter.

In the upper layers, bones of at least four people were found, mixed in with bones of various animals, ranging from deer to raccoons. Beneath that layer were other bones, those of animals that either died out or migrated north at least 10,000 years ago, as the Ice Age glaciers receded and the climate became warmer. These included mammoth, camel, bison, and horses. (Horses were reintroduced to North America by Europeans.)

Today the Deering Estate, the former home of an International Harvester heir, is a county park, and the Cutler Fossil site is protected behind a fence. The closest my wife, Bonnie, and I could get was the porch of the visitor center, from which Sergeant Reed pointed out the location. We probably could have arranged an escort to the site, but the purpose of our visit this day in May 1999 was to find out what the average person could see today of the

Excavators working on Cutler Fossil site after it was saved from pot-hunters. Courtesy Archaeological and Historical Conservancy.

places where the Ancient Miamians had lived. Anyway, I had visited the site when it was being explored.

Bonnie snapped a couple of pictures of the vista, a flat scrubland with the occasional tree jutting out of the palmetto. We thanked Sergeant Reed and got into our car in search of the next Miamians, those 4,000-year-olds who had been until 1985 the first known visitors. Their home was Cheetum Hammock, a tree island in the Everglades, 15 miles away as the condor flew. But we would have to follow the roads and travel five miles farther.

We turned north onto Old Cutler Road at Richmond Drive. As its name implies, the road is old, at least by South Florida standards. The homes represent various eras in the twentieth century, which to most residents is the sum total of the county's history. Cutler Fossil shows that conventional wisdom is off by 9,900 years.

We worked our way north to the Palmetto Expressway via Coral Reef Drive, Palmetto Avenue, SW 104th Street, and Dixie Highway. Just after passing the Dolphin Expressway on the Palmetto, we eased into the right-hand lane for the NW 25th Street ramp. We turned left and crawled west in the heavy industrial-zone traffic, trying in vain to work our way past slow-moving 18-wheelers. Oh, well, our next stop was only a few miles ahead, less than two miles beyond Florida's Turnpike overpass.

The traffic thinned out at 97th Avenue as warehouses gave way to homes on the north side. Soon we saw the overpass and knew our goal was getting nearer. We drove under it . . . and up to a gate blocking the road, flanked by a sign warning of a $500 fine for illegal dumping. The area is being used by Florida Rock Industries, Inc., to mine lime rock for construction fill, and no one is allowed in. Not that it really mattered; twentieth-century drainage has changed the landscape so much that the Cheetum inhabitants wouldn't recognize their home. What was once a sawgrass prairie surrounding their low, teardrop-shaped island is today a barren plain dotted with artificial lakes that mark where the lime rock was removed.

Cheetum Hammock was first examined under the direction of amateur archaeologist Dan D. Laxson in the 1960s, but excavations were not undertaken until 1986. As is often the case in South Florida, it was what is known as salvage archaeology, performed as a legal requirement before an area is developed. In this case the catalyst was the rock mining that continues today.

The excavation was conducted by Christine Newman, then with the Archaeological and Historical Conservancy. The results demonstrated that the site had been occupied for at least 5,000 years by people who allowed the flesh to fall from the bones of the dead before burying the bones and who probably participated in trade networks with groups to the north. Posthole stains indicated the people had homes on the island and probably had a charnel house in which the bodies rested until ready for burial.

The end of the road to Cheetum Hammock, just west of the turnpike on 25th Street. Photo by Bonnie McGoun.

After Bonnie took a couple of pictures of the gate, we turned around and headed back east into the flocks of 18-wheelers. At 87th Avenue we turned south and got onto the Dolphin Expressway. In chronological order our next stop would be the site of a 2,500-year-old fishing village on the east shore of Biscayne Bay, but the site of a not-so-old mound and circle that I expect had ceremonial importance lay on our way across town. I did not feel like backtracking through twentieth-century traffic, so we got off the Dolphin at Lejeune Road and headed south.

When the Dade Circle was photographed from the air in 1925, it still sat in a prairie near the headwaters of the Miami River. By the time Carr surveyed it in 1979, it already was "under fill and urban development," so there were no surprises awaiting us at NW 7th Street, approximately where the circle once was. NW 7th Street also is known as Luis Sabines Way, reflecting the fact that a community in which the first Europeans were Spaniards is once again strongly Hispanic.

I believe the circle, which was nearly 200 feet in diameter, may have been used 1,500 years ago to raise corn for ceremonial purposes. Today, the only thing rising is heat from the asphalt. The four corners are filled with two gasoline stations, a bank building, and an auto-parts store in an old fast-food building. The two highways are filled with cars. The air is filled with exhaust fumes.

As for the mound, the only documentation is a secondhand report by John M. Goggin in his unpublished manuscript on South Florida archaeology. According to Goggin, the mound had been destroyed sometime in the middle 1940s. Even its precise location is unknown. Goggin assumed it was a ceremonial structure because no burials or household garbage were found in it.

I pulled into one of the gasoline stations so Bonnie could take a few more pictures. Then it was back to the Dolphin. We drove east to I-95, north to 125th Street, and east across the Broad Causeway

The Dade Circle today: a sea of automobiles at NW 7th Street and 42nd Avenue. Photo by Bonnie McGoun.

Guarded bridge to a posh island community crosses the mouth of Indian Creek. Photo by Bonnie McGoun.

through Bay Harbor Islands into Surfside. Some 2,500 years ago, fisherfolk built village and burial mounds near the south mouth of Indian Creek, which runs between Bay Harbor Islands and Surfside. Today, the site is covered with asphalt, grass, and upscale homes.

When botanist John Kunkel Small first saw the mounds in 1922, they were within a mangrove swamp. But this was the Roaring Twenties, and the mangroves were doomed. Within a year the land had been filled for development, and the trees were dead. Today, nothing would suggest that anyone had lived here before the twentieth century. The site was roughly between 91st and 94th streets on Bay Drive. The spot at the mouth of Indian Creek where aborigines probably trapped fish now is spanned by a humpback bridge with a police guard shack leading to the exclusive island community of Indian Creek.

After a few more pictures we were on the last leg of our journey, to the mouth of the Miami River. We headed south on Harding Avenue onto Indian Creek Drive, left on 63rd Street to Alton Road and south to the Julia Tuttle Causeway, across the bay to I-95, south to the downtown exit, and east to the U.S. 1 ramp. There we were confronted with giant hotels where humble huts once stood on the north bank of the river. The Ramada Dupont Plaza Hotel sits to the east of the U.S. 1 bridge, the Hyatt to the west with its attached James L. Knight Convention Center.

The sand burial mound that sat on the Dupont Plaza site was destroyed in 1896 for construction of Henry Flagler's Royal Palm Hotel. John M. Goggin reported that 50 to 60 skeletons had been found in the base of the mound. Other burials between the mound and the river reportedly yielded gold ornaments, European pottery, glass beads, and a copper ear plug. Apparently Goggin never saw any of these items, and their whereabouts are unknown.

The Hyatt site fared better. Prior to construction of the convention center, it was excavated. The two-volume report on the Granada site, as it is known because it once was the site of the Granada Apartments, provides a trove of information about the Indians who lived on Biscayne Bay when the Spanish arrived in the sixteenth century. Despite damage from a series of occupations dating back possibly 250 years, the site produced enough information to allow researchers to conclude much about the everyday life of those Indians. My reconstruction in chapter 6 is based in large part on the Granada report.

Our plan was to have dinner in the Dupont Plaza dining room overlooking the river. That would give us a good view of the most famous Miami-Dade County archaeological site ever, the Miami Circle on the south bank. Discovery of the 38-foot-diameter circle in September of 1998 generated worldwide publicity and led to a successful drive to put the 2.2-acre site in public ownership.

Once again, it was a survey prior to construction that led to the find. A developer had planned a $126 million apartment complex on the land, which had once held six small apartment buildings. A septic tank for one of the buildings was found within the circle, which is delineated by a series of holes in the limestone bedrock. While aborigines clearly have occupied the site as long ago as 760 B.C., based on radiocarbon dates, the date of the circle itself has been

The Dupont Plaza Hotel looms where Ancient Miamians
once lived. Photo by William E. McGoun.

questioned. Jerald T. Milanich of the Florida Museum of Natural
History suspects it might be part of the septic system.

For my part, I think the holes held posts for the walls of a circular
temple. A strong piece of evidence is the burial of a shark. It's hard
to see such a burial as being anything except ceremonial; Indians
normally ate the sharks they caught rather than burying them
whole.

Unfortunately, the Dupont Plaza was being remodeled and both
the dining room and the lounge were closed, so Bonnie and I had to
be satisfied with looking through the windows at the Miami Circle.

Reproduction of Indian hut at Arch Creek Park in northern
Miami-Dade County. Photo by Bonnie McGoun.

We wound up instead eating dinner at Wolfie's on Miami Beach,
which has no known prehistoric significance but does have good
food.

The answer to the question "What can the visitor today see of
Miami-Dade County's prehistory?" turned out to be "Not much."
Aside from Cutler Fossil, the only site preserved in a county park is
Arch Creek, at 135th Street and Biscayne Boulevard. We stopped by
on our way to the Surfside site. The park sits atop part of the site,

and a ranger directed us to an area where we could see some seashells brought in by ancient residents. Actually, we saw one shell, sitting near a thatch hut that had just been built by park employees in the style of huts used by the historic Seminole Indians and possibly by the prehistoric inhabitants.

In the following chapters, I hope to give some idea of the everyday life of the people who lived in Miami-Dade County before the Europeans arrived, starting with the group that found Cutler Fossil 10,000 years ago and continuing through the inhabitants of Cheetum Hammock and Surfside, visitors to Dade Circle, and the people who lived at the mouth of the Miami River when the Spanish sailors hove into view.

2

The Ice Age in a Dry Land
(8000 B.C.)

The Man awakened reluctantly, even though the sun was as high as the trees to the east of the campsite. The day before had been a hard one. It had ended in a triumph of sorts, but at a terrible price.

Usually it took relatively little effort to kill one of the small swine (known today as peccaries) that were one of the best sources of food in the area (present-day Miami-Dade County). A band of hunters would hide near one of the small water holes—usually little more than a puddle that was wet only after a rain—that dotted the flat, arid landscape and wait for a band of the animals to approach. The hunters would separate one of the individuals from the pack, preferably a younger one with smaller tusks, and attack it with their stone-tipped wooden spears. As long as the hunters stayed away from the animal's sharp teeth, they were safe, which is one reason they used throwing sticks to give their spears more range and power.

This day, however, things did not go well. In setting the trap, the most important thing is to remain still. Peccaries have poor eye-

It takes a big spear to slay the animals hunted by paleoindians. Oil painting by Theodore Morris, Sarasota, Florida.

sight and will mistake a stationary hunter for a tree. But the beasts also have exceptional hearing. As the hunters were closing in, The Man's nephew coughed.

The beast lunged toward the sound and buried its stiletto-sharp canine teeth into The Nephew's leg. Evidently startled by The Nephew's scream, the peccary released its grip and stepped back. The animal halted, stood still for no more than a second, and then bolted. The Man stayed with his wounded relative while the others ran after the fleeing animal.

The chase had lasted from before noon until nearly sunset. The hunters had no idea how far they had traveled, though they knew they were running toward the descending sun. Every time the peccary slowed and the hunters got nearly close enough to strike, the animal seemed to find some new reserve of strength and race on.

Such is the power of fear. Had they not needed meat so badly, the hunters would have broken off the chase and returned to their camp.

Still, if it had not been for the chase, they never would have found the water. In its panic, the peccary had led the hunters to the edge of a deep hole that opened in an otherwise flat limestone plain. The clump of oak trees, so unlike the low scrub undergrowth that dotted the area, should have told the hunters there was something different here, but they were so intent on pursuing their prey that they paid it no attention.

In fact, The Man's kinsman almost fell into the hole when he abandoned his spear-thrower and, holding the shaft in his hands, lunged at the peccary. The animal sidestepped, and The Kinsman drove his weapon into one of the oaks, snapping its stone point in two. The impact threw him off balance, and he nearly tumbled over the ledge just to the right of the tree.

It was not until after the hunters had cornered and dispatched the peccary that they realized what a wonderful place they had found. Beneath them were ledges at several levels and a small pond at the bottom. This was an extraordinary exception in a land where it rarely rained and most water quickly evaporated.

The hunters certainly were not the first creatures to find the pond. It may have been a favorite spot for the peccaries. The ledges were strewn with bones that the hunters recognized as belonging to various animals they had taken in the past: deer and rabbits and armadillos, skunks and opossums and raccoons. Many smaller animals, not worthy of the hunt, also were represented: shrews, snakes, rats, bats, birds, and toads. What a strange place it was!

Adding another dimension to the scene was the wolf. None of the hunters could say exactly when the wolf appeared, but he had followed them at a distance for some time. Did he hope they would throw him some meat or at least a bone? Or did he have some other reason for being here? Was this pond perhaps a special place for him, a refuge to which unsuspecting animals would repair in search of shade and water, only to become a meal for one of the most efficient of Old Florida predators? This animal, known to scientists today as a dire wolf, was larger than any present-day wolf and was a formidable hunter.

With the arrival of the hunters, however, he was no more than the second most efficient predator. These intruders—unusual two-legged hairless animals—not only had beaten him to a good meal but also had set up camp at the edge of the water hole. He knew he had better keep his distance. He had seen how their spears were able to pierce the peccary's tough hide while the hunters remained out of range of the animal's hooves. One challenged these hairless newcomers at one's peril.

Another danger was the hunters' fire. The wolf had seen fire before, when a bolt of lightning had struck a dry bush. He had investigated and had singed his paw before backing away hastily. Fire was not a thing to embrace. Yet these strange creatures seemed to like it. Further, it had appeared in their midst with no sign of lightning around.

The hunters also were apprehensive. They had seen the big wolves bring down animals with their sharp teeth. They knew the beasts seemed to be afraid of fire, which is one reason the hunters had gathered dry brush and rubbed two sticks together rapidly until the heat ignited the tinder. The task is a tedious one, and it may take a long time before the tinder gets hot enough to set off the fire, but the results are worth the effort. Fire softens meat so it is easier to chew. Fire provides comfort against the chill of the night. And fire keeps wolves at a distance.

The Man stretched and arose. It had been a short night for him, as he had not arrived at the water hole until long after the peccary had been killed. Fortunately, the trail of men and animals was easy to follow. As he walked up to the others, one asked, "How is The Nephew?" The Man lowered his eyes. "He is gone," he said quietly.

The Man had tried desperately to stop the flow of blood from The Nephew's leg, but to no avail. The Nephew groaned as the circle of red in the sand grew. Then he was still, never to make a sound again.

At his full height, The Man was just under six feet tall. Anthropologists ten millennia hence would call him a paleoindian, but that name would have meant nothing to him. For that matter, were a paleoindian to walk through the door today, few would think of him as an Indian. For The Man did not have the broad head and flat face considered typical of Native Americans, but rather a more slender face such as that of Europeans, though he was in fact more closely related to the ancestors of today's Ainu of Japan. Neither did he have the stocky build we associate with Native Americans. His ancestors had reached the New World in one of the first migrations across the Bering land bridge from Asia, formed when lower sea levels exposed the ocean floor, whereas later Native Americans represent more recent migrations.

It was going to be another busy day. By the time the hunters had killed the peccary, it was too near dark to butcher it. They had cut off chunks of meat and roasted them over the fire on sticks for their dinner, but now they had to cut up the animal into portions that could be carried back to camp. The best portion went to The Man's uncle, the head of the hunting party, whose knowledge of the peccary's habits was the source of great admiration. Next came the portions for those who had actually speared the animal. The Man's kinsman was included in this group even though his spear had missed. Then came the rest of the hunters, including The Man.

Once the meat was cut, using the edges of the stone spear points as knives, the hunters packed up for the long walk home. The Kinsman retrieved the broken piece of his spear point; he intended to refashion it into some form of cutter. Spear-point fragments were far too precious to discard. This particular point had been obtained in trade from another band that needed meat, and the Kinsman had no idea where to find the hard rock (we would call it chert) from which it was fashioned. He had heard of a land to the north where this rock was plentiful, but he had no idea how to get there.

It had taken the person who made the point a considerable time to set a fire to break off a chunk of a boulder, then chip away at that chunk with a piece of bone, shaping it and then giving it a sharp edge suitable for spearing or cutting. Shallow grooves on either side of the base accepted the cordage that held the point to the spear and made the hafting more secure. (Archaeologists would later call the style of such points Dalton.) The spear itself was a length of straight oak branch trimmed of bark and smoothed with one of the cutting tools.

A new spear itself presented difficulties, mainly due to the scarcity of suitable limbs, but that was nothing compared with the problems in replacing a broken point. It would take The Kinsman a long time to make the broken-off piece usable again. But for some things, a person simply must find the time.

Similar chert objects, more elongated than the spear points, would serve as needles, and chunks of the rock barely modified would do as scrapers; both were used to convert the skins of animals into clothing. The hunters would make cutting and scraping tools from the local limestone, treating them with fire to make them harder, but still these were greatly inferior to objects fashioned of chert. Limestone also was shaped into balls that would be tied together in pairs with lengths of woven fiber to make throwing objects, useful for snaring small animals though ineffective against peccaries. Another good weapon against small animals was a nonreturning boomerang fashioned from an oak limb with another limb joining it at a right angle. Other objects, including pins and awls and needles, were made of animal bone, and many more of wood. Wooden pins often were carved in the shape of animals.

The sun was nearly overhead before the hunters began walking toward the point at which it had appeared that day. They drank their fill of water before starting, knowing that they might find nothing else to drink before reaching the camp. The Miami of 10,000 years ago was a far different world. Rains came rarely, and there were no rivers. Also, the sea was 100 feet lower than today, which meant the shoreline was several miles east of Key Biscayne. The water hole was near today's Old Cutler Road. It was going to be a long walk.

The sand reflected the heat. There was no shade. But the hunters were used to this sort of life, and they walked swiftly. The Man's uncle assured them that if they kept going in the same direction, remembering that the sun would pass over their heads and then be behind them, they would find the salty water and then the camp. The other men had faith in The Man's uncle, and they followed him.

The sun was perhaps halfway to the horizon behind them when they came upon The Nephew's body. The Man had covered it with rocks to keep animals away. The hunters removed the rocks. The Man grabbed The Nephew's shoulders while another hunter grabbed his legs. They lifted him between them and resumed their trek eastward.

The sun had nearly set when the hunters heard the surf. They crested a small dune and saw the water. Then they heard, off to the left, laughter. It was children playing at the camp, which was no more than a quarter mile north of where they had reached the shore. There was still a bit of light when they arrived.

The Woman smiled with pride as The Man approached with his share of the meat. The Boy and The Girl ran up. It was a special occasion, for hunting was not a sure thing. Often the men would return with nothing but unsatisfied appetites. Then the people would have to keep on eating whatever they could pull from the plants, or perhaps small animals that scurried in the brush. Scientists 10,000 years later would call these people big-game hunters, but they did not see themselves that way. They ate whatever they could catch or harvest, though big animals were to be prized for the amount of meat they provided and as a means of demonstrating the hunters' skill.

The Man had heard stories of animals far larger than anything he had ever seen, of giant hairy creatures with long teeth that could impale an unwary hunter. But he had never seen one of these creatures, which would become known as mammoths, for they had already died out. One story in particular told of a band of hunters that formed an arc around one of the giant animals, leaving open only a pathway leading to a hole in the ground such as the one these hunters had just found. Once they were in place, the ancient hunters shouted and waved their hands until the beast began running in the only direction without one of these strange creatures in its way.

The hunters had chosen their positions well, and the beast reacted as expected, racing blindly until it fell into the hole. Once it stopped thrashing, the hunters were able to dispatch it with their spears while staying safely out of the way of its tusks.

The hunt did not always go that well. If the hunters were not correctly positioned, or if the animal did not react as expected, the beast might escape to one side or the other of the hole. Or, worse, it might charge at one of the hunters, either trampling him or impaling him. This is why before every hunt the men asked the spirit of the mammoth to cooperate so they would have meat to eat and hides to wear and bones from which to make tools.

Had The Man or one of his companions dug into the ground at the new water hole, they would have learned that the long-ago hunt of which they had heard was held at this very spot. They would have found bones of the mammoth, along with those of horses, camels, and bison. But they had no reason to dig, so they didn't.

People in future years would compensate for the loss of the meat-bearers by tapping the bounty of the oceans, rich in both fish and shellfish. But those of The Man's generation did not yet know

To paleoindians, the ocean was a novelty but of no subsistence value. Oil painting by Theodore Morris, Sarasota, Florida.

how to exploit those riches. The shore along which they had camped was for them a novel environment but not a useful one; once their curiosity was satisfied, they would soon move on, never to return. The water tasted terrible, and they knew nothing of the creatures that lived offshore. In this dry, different Miami-Dade, hunger was often their lot.

While the men hunted, the women gathered—mostly nuts, seeds, and roots, with the occasional wild fruits. The Woman had an oaken mortar and pestle with which she would grind the nuts so they could be made into porridge. Plant foods were the most important part of the people's diet because they remained edible for some time after they were gathered.

Meat was another matter. Quickly—that is, as quickly as their technology would allow—a fire was kindled, and big chunks of meat were roasted on sticks in the flame. The hunters ate first, then the women and children and old men. They ate until they could eat no more, because there was no purpose in saving meat. After a few days it would be unsafe to eat. The people had heard stories of how ancestors had sickened and died after eating old meat, and they had enough faith in the stories not to test them.

The Boy asked again, as he had many times, when he could join the hunt. When you are big enough, The Man told him, as he had each time before. The Boy had lived only six years, though The Man could not have expressed it this way. Aside from sunrise and sunset, there was virtually no way to note from the weather the passage of time. There was no rainy season and very little temperature variation from summer to winter. The Man could have noticed how the sunrise and sunset points move north and south during the course of the year, but it would be hard for nomads to recognize the differences and in any case they would have had no reason to do so. In fact, they would have had no reason to think about, or talk about, the weather, as it rarely changed.

What The Man did know was that The Boy was neither an infant nor an adolescent. When he reached the latter stage, he would be strong enough to share in the hunt. Until then he would continue to chase rodents with little sticks, pretending they were peccaries and he was a man.

The Girl, born two years before The Boy, knew she would never be a hunter. Instead, she would continue to help The Woman and learn the things women must do. She would collect food and plant fibers. She would weave bags to carry what she had collected, snares to catch small animals, and mats for sleeping and for protection from sun and wind. She would clean animal skins and stitch them into clothing with bone needles and fiber thread. She would make digging sticks from oak branches and use those sticks to dig up edible roots.

When The Man was in camp, The Boy would help him fashion other oak boughs into spears. Or he would listen as the men told of hunts past and dreamed of hunts to come. For hunting was the way

Children spent much of their time practicing the roles they would fill as adults. Oil painting by Theodore Morris, Sarasota, Florida.

a man defined himself, and courage was a great virtue. This is why the big, and therefore dangerous, animals were so important even though they provided only a small part of the family's food. In fact, that share was becoming smaller, for the number of big animals was declining. If the old tales were to be believed, the rains were coming more often and the sun was getting hotter. Also, there seemed to be more bands competing for the food.

This evening, the men had a new subject: that marvelous water hole. Would it not be better to live there? From the number of bones, it must be a popular place for all sorts of animals. They could become great hunters once more, able to feed their families without needing to make constant overnight trips in search of game or water. There was enough to eat that they could join forces with the other bands from which they found mates for their youngsters.

They could live on one of the ledges within the hole, with fresh water only an arm's length away.

It was settled. The Man's uncle said so, and the rest agreed.

When morning came, the hunters carried The Nephew's body into the surf. They lay it in the water, placed a woven plant-fiber mat over it, and secured the mat with a ring of rocks. As the hunters did their sad work, the women stood on the shore chanting a simple tune expressing their sorrow and asking the powers that controlled their life to see that The Nephew would be happy and fulfilled wherever he now was.

Once the burial ceremony was finished, the people packed up their possessions and retraced the route of the hunt. It was going to be a very good day.

3

Seizing the Opportunities
(2000 B.C.)

It was time to bury The Leader. He had lain in the charnel house for more than the time necessary for one moon to be replaced by another, and nothing was left except his bones, which were becoming brittle. Now the people of the tree island could lay him to rest properly. It was up to The Man to see that all the requirements of their religion, passed down from one generation to the next since far in the mists of the past, were fulfilled. Otherwise, there would be no rest for The Leader, and his spirit would roam the earth.

The Man approached his task with confidence. He knew these ceremonies well. After all, The Leader was his father and had been in charge of the ceremonies for many others. The people of the tree island were egalitarian, and there was no difference in burial traditions whether the deceased was an old woman or a young boy, a great hunter or a poor one.

The Man had taken over leadership on the tree island not because he was The Leader's son but because he was wise in the ways of his people. He had been the chief assistant when his father was in charge of the deer hunt, a leadership role he now assumed along

Spear at the ready, this man seeks turtle in shallow water near a tree-island. Oil painting by Theodore Morris, Sarasota, Florida.

with his chores as leader of the village. Thus he knew where to find the fish and the animals that sustained the people's bodies. He also had learned from his father the religious lore that sustained their souls. He knew all there was to know in his world.

Elsewhere, great pyramids were being built in a place called Egypt and great palaces on an island called Crete, but these wonders were beyond not only his knowledge but also his ability to imagine. People living 4,000 years in the future would call The Man an Archaic Indian, but that also would have had no meaning for him. He was simply a human being, the leader of the only people he knew.

Despite his knowledge, he could not order anything to be done; he could only suggest and cajole until there was consensus among the men of the island. Usually that was an easy task, for most decisions were dictated by the nature of the environment. The women would harvest the many fruits on the island—figs, black cherries, persimmons, hackberries, mulberries, palm berries—and snare

Villagers roast an alligator at a village on an Everglades tree island. Art by Merald Clark, courtesy of Institute of Archaeology and Paleoenvironmental Studies, University of Florida.

small animals with plant-fiber loops attached to wooden handles. The men would pole their dugout canoes into the surrounding waters in search of fish to catch in fiber nets or turtles to impale with wooden spears tipped with deer bone. When they found an uninhabited island, they would alight to snare small animals, usually rabbits.

The alligator was a tempting target because it provided a lot of meat and a tough hide—an ideal material for making containers stitched together with plant fiber or sinew. But that tough hide made the animal extremely difficult to kill; the hunter would have to leap upon the beast and stab it in its soft underside with a stone-tipped knife. One slip and the hunter would become the prey, his bones shattered by the alligator's massive jaws and his flesh torn by its claws. Unless they were desperate for food, or the animal seemed weak, the hunters generally would leave the alligator alone.

Aside from burial ceremonies, The Man's most important duty was to lead the hunt, which required more teamwork than any other activity. The hunt was usually held at those times when the air was getting cooler and the water was at its highest level, forcing the deer to retreat to high ground where they could more easily be brought down with spears hurled with throwing sticks.

The deer provided more meat than any other animal, but their importance went far beyond mere food. Their skins, scraped of hair and fat and dried over a fire, provided both the simple wrappings the people wore around their loins and the bags for carrying what the men hunted and the women gathered. The bones of the deer provided both points for the spears and the hooks by which the base of the spear fitted into the spear-thrower, as well as scrapers to remove the hair from the skin and needles with which to sew garments and bags together.

But the deer were not that easy to hunt. Even when forced onto tree islands by rising water, they could dart to and fro swiftly, evading spears. A successful hunt required teamwork, putting a premium on The Man's knowledge of deer habits. The hunt was the only occasion when The Man's orders were obeyed without question, for there was no time to discuss matters and reach a consensus when pursuing a speedy animal.

The deer was so important that it occupied a special place in the belief system of the tree-island people. One of The Man's duties was to petition the spirit of the deer to allow the hunters to succeed so the people could have food and clothing and tools. If several hunts failed, the men could depose their leader and pick a new one by consensus. That was how The Man's father had become leader.

The only other large land animal also occupied a place of honor, but for different reasons. The bear was not really an animal and not really a human being, but rather a special being with some of the powers of each. One of the tales passed down through the generations until The Man's time concerns the period when bears were plentiful and spoke with humans. One day the bears decided they would no longer talk, perhaps because the humans had offended their spirits.

The bears on occasion would stand on two legs, as do the humans, but most of the time they would lumber about on all fours. They would allow the humans to kill them for hide and meat, provided their spirits had been properly honored beforehand, but there were so few bears left that hunting parties might go for years without seeing one. As with the deer, the best time to hunt the bear was when the water was high and the air was getting cooler, for the animal would be heavier in this season and could not run as quickly.

Occasionally, during the cooler part of the year, the men would travel to the coast and wade in the shallows. Besides netting fish, they would collect conch, from the shells of which they would fashion tools, and clams, which provided a food treat. But most of the time they found all they wanted close at hand.

The exception was during those times when the water level had fallen so low that fires had destroyed the plants bearing fruits and the deer were able to evade the hunters by running across dry land that otherwise would have been too wet. These times would test The Man's powers of persuasion. He would have to convince his peers to change their routine and roam farther in search of food. Change does not come easily to people of settled habits, and often it would take days and nights of nonstop talking for The Man to get others to see the situation his way. Sometimes he could not prevail even then, the others preferring to take their chances closer to home and family.

Fortunately, times of want were rare, due to the nature of the people's home environment. The island and its environs were two different worlds, even though the highest point on the island was

Villager kindles a fire on the edge of a tree island overlooking Everglades saw grass. Oil painting by Theodore Morris, Sarasota, Florida.

only six feet or so above the water. The island was largely covered with trees such as oak, maple, gumbo-limbo, and tamarind, while the surrounding waters were filled with saw grass.

The island was an ideal place to live for several reasons. It afforded high-and-dry living with easy access to the water and its resources. The island also was immune to many of the natural disasters that often ravaged its surroundings. The Man remembered one occasion when a dry-season saw grass fire roared down upon the island from the north. The Man, then a young boy, was frightened, but his father, who was wise in the ways of saw grass fire, told the people not to fear. Suddenly, as it reached the edge of the island, the fire parted and circled around the island. The litter beneath the island's trees had retained enough moisture that it would not ignite.

The island also was not affected by the strange white death that sometimes descended on the saw grass on those rare occasions when it was very cold. And the trees deflected the howling winds that occasionally roared across the saw grass after a strange time of stillness near the end of the hot months. All in all, it was a good place to live.

As The Man waited for daybreak, he remembered many of the stories his father used to tell in the evenings after a hunt. His favorite was of a time far, far in the past (maybe 3,000 years, to use a term of no meaning to The Man) when The Leader's ancestors bested The Slender People in a great battle.

When The Ancestors trekked south into Florida, they found people already there, people who were taller than they but not as stoutly built. Their faces were longer and narrower than the wide face of The Ancestors, and their noses were more prominent. The Slender People spoke strange words The Ancestors could not understand. Nevertheless, by their gestures The Slender People made it clear they took pride in their great prowess in killing giant animals. This puzzled The Ancestors, because there were no giant animals to kill.

The Slender People persisted in using spears with stone tips that were too large for the animals that did exist. Also, The Slender People had no idea of how to harvest food from the sea. In fact, they were nothing but nuisances as far as The Ancestors were concerned. Things came to a head one day when the two groups went after the same deer. The Slender People could not kill it; their presence merely scared it off so no one could get it.

The Ancestors talked about their problem long into the night. Finally, they reached a consensus on a course of action. Before dawn they sneaked up on The Slender People's camp and fell upon them before they could reach their weapons, dispatching them quickly. Never again would they have to put up with these pests who talked a good hunt but couldn't carry one out.

The Man's other favorite tale concerned the discovery of the island. The Ancestors had spent many years along the shore of what newcomers far in the future would call Biscayne Bay. The men

Brickell Bluff formation today, along Bayshore Drive near Coconut Grove. Photo by William E. McGoun.

made occasional hunting forays into the interior pinelands, but for the most part they collected shellfish for food and for tools, while the women combed the nearby hammocks for cocoplums, pigeon plums, pond apples, marlberries, and acorns.

But then a strange thing happened. The waters began to rise. The Ancestors moved their huts several times, until they were pinned against the low cliffs known in years to come as the Brickell Bluffs, and still the waters advanced. They could not move atop the bluffs, because other people already lived there. What were they to do?

The Leader of that time saw only one solution: go west. It took days and days of discussion to reach a consensus on the move. Many of The Ancestors preferred to stay on land they knew. After all, the water might stop rising. If it rose, could it not also fall? Wasn't it better to see what would happen than to strike out for an unknown land?

One by one, however, the others came around. The Leader had proven himself wise many times in the past. And there was no arguing with the fact that it was getting increasingly difficult to find enough to eat where they were. The pain of hunger has a way of driving out the fear of the unknown. Finally, the last holdout agreed to move, entrusting to The Leader the task of guiding them.

The Ancestors abandoned their huts, taking only a few tools and some woven bags full of berries. They went across the bluffs, through the woodlands, and into open grasslands. The people living on the bluffs watched them with apprehension, lest they seek a share of food supplies that were barely adequate for the bluff-dwellers. But The Leader had planned well, and there were enough berries to sustain The Ancestors until they moved beyond the bluff-dwellers.

By picking his way carefully, The Leader guided the party through water shallow enough so even the children could wade. But they could not live in such country indefinitely. Some nights, they had to camp on damp ground. The Leader was nearly ready to turn back, even if it meant fighting other groups for a choice living site, when he saw the island. It was dry, and it was vacant. The Ancestors had found a new home.

They would discover how to exploit their new surroundings, learning some skills from people they met at another tree island to the south and figuring out others for themselves. Most important, they learned how to turn a log into a watercraft so they could travel without wading. Also, they would teach the inland people some skills, such as the techniques for netting fish and gathering shellfish. Soon the inland people began visiting the coast on occasion to put their newfound knowledge to work.

Now, however, it was time for The Man to set aside thoughts of the past and to get on with burying The Leader. As soon as the sun had risen over the saw grass to the east, The Man saw that everyone on the island was awake. After a meal of berries and rabbit meat, he assembled the people in the clearing amid their simple open wooden huts on the northern, wider end of the teardrop-shaped island. The mist that had hung over the saw grass at daybreak had vanished. It was a clear day, so clear that The Man could imagine that he was seeing forever into the distance. On such days The Man would have understood why people far in the future would call this land the Everglades.

Once the people were assembled, The Man led a procession to the charnel platform near the south end of the island. There they gathered while he petitioned all those who had predeceased The Leader to welcome him among them. Then the bones were carefully removed from the platform and carried farther south to where two young men, chosen by The Man for their prowess in the hunt, had dug a hole in the ground.

As the others watched, The Man took his hatchet, made from the lip of a queen conch shell hafted on a tree limb and held in place with deer sinews, and began to break the long bones apart. They had to be broken, or else The Leader's soul would be forever imprisoned within them. Once The Man was finished, he carefully placed the bones on an animal skin that he then tied into a bundle. He lowered the bundle into the hole, and the two young men covered it with the rich dark soil of the island. Then the Man led another supplication to those who had died before.

These ceremonies were so important that they would be performed for any member of the group, no matter what the other demands on the people's time. Enemies were another matter. When The Ancestors killed The Slender People, they left the bodies where they fell. On the infrequent occasions when the people of the tree island fought with residents of another island, the enemies were buried immediately without ceremony.

The people living near the coast also followed similar ceremonies, except that they did not break the bones prior to burial. When burying enemies, they cut off the hands and feet first so the foes could never again walk into their territory or carry a weapon.

With the ceremonies successfully concluded, the people returned to the village for a day of ease. There would be no hunting or fishing or gathering this day, no fashioning of tools or weapons from shell or wood or bone. It would be a day of eating and remembering.

A special responsibility had fallen to The Man. Now it was he who would have to keep alive the memories, to tell succeeding generations how The Ancestors had vanquished The Slender People and how they had found the island. It was he who would have to convince the other men when circumstances dictated a change in their routine or to reassure them when they had doubts that the spirits were with them.

The burial ceremonies had gone well, and The Man had come away from them with satisfaction. He was now even more sure he could preserve the group's heritage, just as had his father and the many leaders who had gone before.

4

Harvesting the Bounty of the Sea (500 B.C.)

It was barely getting light in the east, but everyone in the village already was awake. The Woman had seen to that. As soon as she had awakened, she went to each of the thatch huts along the side of the shallow stream and roused everyone inside.

Why? Because all the signs said this would be a great day to capture what the people of the village called the fat fish and people 2,500 years later would call the black drum. This was the time of year, as the days became longer and the nights shorter, that the fat fish would swim into the stream to eat the shelled animals that lived on the bottom. The Woman had been watching the water for days, and every day it seemed the number of fat fish was increasing.

Also, the moon had been round the night before, rising as the sun set and setting as the sun rose. The Woman knew this meant the water would rise higher than normal that day, peaking shortly after the sun passed nearly overhead. The fat fish would race into the stream on the rising current and race back out on the falling current late in the day.

The people of the village could capture a lot of the fat fish that day by driving poles into the streambed near its mouth and weaving limbs around the poles to form a pair of barriers in a V pattern pointing up the creek, with a narrow opening between them. The fat fish would find their way upstream easily, as the current would push them toward the opening, but the afternoon current would push them away from the opening as they tried to leave the stream, their bellies full of meat from the animals that people living long afterward would call oysters.

The people could have constructed the barriers earlier, but there always seemed to be something else to do. The village was a marvelous place to live, with food seemingly asking to be harvested both on the land and in the water. The spirits found within every living thing clearly smiled on the villagers. The Woman came in for her share of the credit. After all, had not the people prospered under her leadership?

From the time she was a little girl, The Woman had learned from her mother, the previous village leader, how to identify the signs that told when certain foods were at their best, and to recognize the warning signals of the fierce storms that sometimes lashed the island on which the village sat during the time of year when the days were getting shorter and the nights longer. When her mother died during the last storm season, it was understood that The Woman would take charge, beginning with the ceremonies held as the mother's bones were laid to rest in the burial mound north of the village. Like the people of the tree island, the people of the fat fish set out the dead until the flesh fell from the bones before burial.

On second thought, the phrase "take charge" is perhaps a bit too strong. For the villagers operated on consensus. The Woman could advise, and her words were given great weight due to her knowledge, but she could not force anyone to do anything against his or her will.

A woman returns to her village with a basket of fruit. Oil painting by Theodore Morris, Sarasota, Florida.

The storm season also was the time of year when the villagers devoted as much time as possible to gathering the fruits of the trees around the village. Cocoplums, sea grapes, pigeon plums, cabbage palms, saw palmettos, mulberries, figs, prickly pears—all were ripe for the picking. Another good source of plant food was the sprouts of the red mangrove that grew in the water at the edge of the stream, but they could be gathered throughout the year.

The season when days were the shortest was best for gathering the roots that people living far in the future would call coontie. These roots provided a nourishing starch usually eaten in a sort of porridge, but a lot of work was involved in their preparation. The roots had to be pounded into pulp, soaked in a water-filled wooden trough, and squeezed to force out the starch, which then was allowed to dry into a yellowish white solid. All of this was necessary

Mangroves along the bay were a source of nutrition at any season. Courtesy Florida State Archives.

because otherwise the substance would make anyone who ate it terribly ill, if not dead. The Woman did not know how her ancestors learned all of this, but the knowledge had been passed from mother to daughter for many years.

Besides being a source of food, trees provided the poles and sticks for the fish barriers, the shafts of spears, the poles and thatch for homes. Tree bark or palm leaves yielded the fiber for mats and nets, for sacks to tote fruit, as well as for the breechcloths that constituted the people's only clothing.

The land also provided animals that furnished both food and raw material for tools. There were turtles, dogs, minks, rabbits, pumas, foxes, opossums, otters, lynxes, two types of deer, and raccoons. The deer were particularly prized because they supplied a lot of meat as well as sturdy bones for fishhooks, needles, pins, knives, spear points, and ornaments. The villagers would pursue the deer with spears, using nets for most other animals. The slow-moving turtles were simply grabbed and picked up by hand. Nets also were used on occasion to catch the birds—loons, pelicans, cormorants, egrets— that came to eat fruit from the trees or fish from the water, though snaring a bird was very difficult.

The most difficult resource to obtain was drinking water. The villagers could get some fresh water from shallow holes dug in the higher ground to the east of their homes, but sand kept collapsing into the holes. The water would be carried back to the village in deerskin bags. Due to the scarcity, it was used sparingly. One of The Woman's more difficult duties was advising the people on how much they could drink and when. Sometimes it would take hours of discussion to reach a consensus.

A long time before The Woman's day (about 1,500 years earlier), people to the north and to the west had begun making superior containers for water and food by forming clay into bowl shapes and heating it until it became hard. But The Woman had not heard of this, and her people continued to use deerskin bags.

The land, however, could not compare with the sea when it came to nourishing the people. The waters near the village were a paradise of wonderful things to eat. The same oysters the drum craved were a favorite of the villagers. So were the conch, which also provided hard shells from which the villagers would fashion ax heads (hafted to sticks with plant fibers or sinews), awls to work animal skins, hammers, ornaments, and even net weights.

And then there were the fish, so many varieties of them that virtually no one but The Woman knew them all, and she had had a lifetime of concentrating on such things. The waters near the village were home to sheepshead, sea catfish, channel bass, jack, toadfish, mullet, and sea trout, to use names The Woman never heard. While some species, notably the catfish, were landed with bone hooks attached to fiber lines, most were caught in nets, either small nets wielded by a lone fisherman and held down with stone or shell weights or larger nets fastened between two poles to intercept a swimming school of fish. If buoyancy was needed, seed pods or gourds would be affixed to the netting.

The ocean just beyond the ridge to the east of the village was alive with sharks, tarpon, and sailfish, but the villagers rarely tried to catch them there. For one thing, there was plenty of food closer to home. For another, ocean fishing was dangerous, what with storms and the strength of the ocean fish themselves. In any case, ocean fish occasionally wandered into the lagoon into which the shallow stream emptied, and they could be encircled by a group of villagers and forced ashore.

When such a fish fell into their hands, it provided not only a lot of meat but also the raw material for tools. Shark teeth had the hardest cutting edge available, while stingray spines and billfish snouts made excellent spear points. Fish vertebrae were fashioned into ear ornaments.

But the real prize was the fat fish. Some of them weighed as much as a man, though most were lighter. Even so, they were relatively massive (averaging 50 pounds). Each fat fish yielded a large supply of good meat, not to mention bones for tools.

On this day, when there were a lot of fat fish in the shallow stream, it would take a lot of work to harvest them, but the rewards would make it worthwhile.

After a morning meal of dried fish and fruit, The Woman put the villagers to work. The poles for the barriers already had been set in place as The Woman had indicated, and some sticks already had been collected, but more would be needed to complete the trap. The Woman directed other village women to gather additional sticks as the men wove the collected sticks among the poles, beginning at the edges of the stream and working toward the center. With many hands at work, the task went quickly. By the time the women arrived with more sticks, the ones on hand were already in place.

Villagers gather fish at a weir placed in a creek near their village. Art by Merald Clark, courtesy of Institute of Archaeology and Paleoenvironmental Studies, University of Florida.

The Woman watched carefully as the barriers rose higher out of the water. They had to be high enough so fish wouldn't escape over them at high water, but making them any higher would be a waste of time and effort. The Woman knew how high the water would rise this day and therefore how high the barriers must be. When each section reached the proper height, she signaled the men to begin building the next section.

As the men worked, the fat fish already were making their way into the stream on the rising water. The men did not stop to catch the fish; there would be time for that later. Their efforts early in the day were better directed toward putting the barriers in place. Shortly before the sun reached its highest point in the sky, the task was completed to The Woman's satisfaction. Now it was time to have another meal of fish and fruit, and to wait.

The sun was more than halfway to the western horizon when the water began to churn. The fat fish were trying to return to the open water of the lagoon. A few got through the opening between the barriers, but most were herded toward one shore or the other. When enough of the fat fish were clustered near each shore, The Woman signaled for the harvest to begin.

The men and some of the women and children were divided into two groups, one for each barrier. They waded into the water barehanded. There would be no need for either fishhook or net. The waders simply grabbed the fat fish and carried them to shore. The other women and children, also divided into a group for each barrier, waited. They let the fat fish squirm until they were dead. Then they went to work with conch-shell knives, separating the flesh from the bones and setting the flesh out to dry.

It was nearly dark when the last of the fat fish were harvested and cleaned. The people were exhausted, and many bore scratches from the fins of the fat fish. But no one minded. It had been a wonderful harvest. There was enough meat to sustain the villagers for weeks. They could relax and take it easy and simply enjoy living in paradise.

But first, there would be a grand feast. The women took sticks left over from the barriers and built a fire, lighting it by rubbing two sticks together until the heat turned to flame. More sticks were used to build a rack over the flames, onto which fish fillets were set to roast. Everyone—man, woman, child—ate until they could eat no more.

After the feast, The Woman led the traditional round of storytelling. The tales were familiar, but the people enjoyed them all the same. It was The Woman's first time leading the discussion, but she performed flawlessly. After all, she had listened carefully to her mother during many such feasts.

The most popular story was how the villagers' ancestors had found this special place and learned how to harvest its bounty. The

Woman had no idea how many seasons had passed since that day, but twenty-first-century scientists know it couldn't have been more than 500 years, because the barrier island didn't exist until roughly 1100 B.C. and it would have taken some time for vegetation to become established.

At any rate, according to the traditional story, The Ancestors were sleeping one night in a temporary camp near the water, when the spirit of the fat fish came to their leader in a dream and told him how to build the barriers so the fish could offer themselves to the villagers. More likely, a storm-felled tree had created a natural trap, and some ancestor of the villagers had noticed the results and realized people could build barriers when and where they wished. But the villagers preferred their version. It gave them a feeling that life was not beyond their control, that by performing the proper ceremonies to appeal to the spirit of the fat fish they would prosper.

After all, the fat fish had made it possible for them to live in one place virtually year-round. They cut a canal so they could bring their dugout canoes up to the edge of the area upon which they built their homes, simple huts of pine logs and palmetto thatch. Over time the homesites would be higher as the people built up the land with shells and sand, in part to stay ahead of rising waters.

When they did leave, for a fishing foray in the ocean or to collect fruit that did not grow near the village, they often were gone just for the day, returning to their huts at nightfall. That was quite an improvement over the lives of The Ancestors, most of whom had to keep constantly on the move in search of food and could never have a structure as permanent as the village huts or the amount of possessions—tools, utensils, ornaments—the villagers had amassed. It made the villagers feel good to believe this bounty was the result of their wise actions and not of mere chance.

A permanent village also was important in a spiritual sense, in that it gave them a better way to honor the spirits of The Ancestors. Before they settled down, the villagers had carried the skulls of their dead with them in their wanderings. Once they had built a permanent camp for the living, they also could build a permanent camp for the dead. North of the village they placed the skulls—19 of them, though the villagers could not express such a number—on a cleared patch of ground and covered them with sand brought in from higher ground nearer the ocean. This in turn was covered with clay and then with more sand.

By The Woman's time, the second sand layer was being used for burials. At first, the villagers had buried people soon after death simply by laying them in the sand and covering them. Later they would bend their legs to make a more compact bundle and still later would set the bodies out until the flesh had fallen away and then bury the bones. It was in this manner that The Woman had buried her mother, after setting a fire beside the bones to help the spirit of her mother rise free.

Most of the dead had succumbed to the ravages of old age, but some had fallen in battle. Occasionally, a group of wanderers would stumble upon the village and try to take over. The villagers, having grown in number after settling down, were always able to fend off these challenges, but not without paying a price. There had been no such battles during The Woman's time or that of her mother. Perhaps the prowess of the villagers in protecting their home had become so well known that no one felt ready to challenge them.

Ceremonies for the dead were no small matter. After all, The Ancestors had found this wonderful place, had defended it against challengers, and had obtained the permission of the fat fish to take them and use their flesh and bones. The excellent diet allowed the children to grow into strong and robust adults, though the grit in their food took its toll on their teeth as they grew older. Often, all of the rear grinding teeth would be lost with advanced age. Still, tooth wear and pain had been a problem even before they settled down, and the sedentary life brought many benefits. It was only fitting that the present-day villagers show respect to those to whom they owed so much.

The round moon was nearly overhead when the stories ended and the villagers went to their huts to sleep. It would be a comfortable sleep, for it had been a wonderful day. The spirit of the fat fish clearly was pleased. So were the villagers.

5

Tame Plants and Hard Earth
(A.D. 500)

The Man arose slowly. The sun was just rising in the direction of the great water, and it was still and muggy in the pine prairie where The Man and the rest of his people had camped for several days. He was not afraid, but he was apprehensive. A great weight lay upon his shoulders, for this was the day he must decide if The Wild One was to live or die.

The Man was the keeper of the medicine bundle, a deerskin in which objects with powers to cure were wrapped inside smaller pieces of skin. People living 1,500 years later would call him a medicine man or shaman, but that did not do justice to his role in society. His interpretation of the objects determined what the people must do to make sure the tame plants would grow and produce small pods of tasty kernels that people in the future would call corn. He would say when and where some of those kernels should be buried so there would be more plants in the next season of hot and rainy days. He was also the steward of the knowledge of how to supplicate the spirits so the dead would rest in peace.

The Man had prepared for his role ever since he could remember. When he was but a boy, the men of the village had noticed that he possessed the qualities of boldness and thoughtfulness needed in a keeper. The old keeper, a distant cousin, had taken The Man as his apprentice, showing him how each ceremony must be conducted so that the spirits would smile on the people and allow them to prosper.

Keepers of the medicine bundle traditionally came from his village, located where the sweet water meets the salty water. (One thousand years later, this village would be known as Tequesta.) The Man's village—roughly five miles east of the campsite, to use terms that would have meant nothing to The Man—was so honored because it was the center of religious life for the surrounding area.

On the south shore of what people much later would call the Miami River, across from their homes, the villagers had built a large circular hut with a wood floor and entrances on the east, south, and west. Construction had been laborious. To make the structure stable, the villagers had drilled a circle of holes in the limestone bedrock using sharpened wooden sticks. Into these holes they had placed columns on which rested rafters that in turn supported the thatch roof.

Inside this building, ceremonies were held to honor the dead and to propitiate the spirits that the villagers believed dwelled in every object, alive or not. The building was so large—40 times as long as a human foot from side to side—that the entire village could assemble within, with room left over for visitors.

There was, however, one time of year when the village was not the center of the people's universe, a time when his role as keeper of the medicine bundle put a special burden on The Man. His first great test would come this day, the climactic day of the annual ceremonies of thanks for the tasty kernels. The ceremonies were held each year when the moon died in the eastern sky at the start of the

Villagers from all over today's Miami-Dade County gathered once a year. Art by Merald Clark, courtesy of Institute of Archaeology and Paleoenvironmental Studies, University of Florida.

hot and rainy season. The old leader had taken ill suddenly and died at the end of the last ceremonies, and the people of The Man's village had accepted The Man as his successor with almost no discussion, a sign of their respect for his skills.

The task this year had been especially arduous. Instead of returning to the same ceremonial ground the people had used since before The Man could remember, the people had had to construct a new ground some distance from the old one. Clearly the old site had lost the ability to protect the people. If the keeper of the bundle had died there, no one was safe.

It was the fifth day of the ceremonies. The first day had been devoted to setting up the grounds in the piney woods near the source of the sweet-water stream that emptied into the salty water near The Man's village. A large circle had been cleared and cleaned, and logs for a fire stacked in its center. An open thatched hut had been set up near the west end of the circle and another fire, for The Man to use in his ceremonies, at the east end. Clusters of huts, scattered through the woods, had been built for people from the various villages who had gathered for this most important of times. The people had other ceremonies, especially when they buried their dead, but those paled in importance before what people in the distant future would call the Green Corn Ceremony.

Near the circle was a tall pole made from a pine sapling stripped of its limbs. Each afternoon during the ceremonies, the children played a game in which teams representing different villages would try to hit the pole with a ball made of deer hide stuffed with deer hair.

On the second day, the men had sat in the open hut, inhaling the smoke of burning plants. They had used special objects made of hardened earth with a bowl sitting atop a platform. They had fashioned the objects by forming earth into the same shape as a stone smoking device obtained many years earlier from far to the north, then burying it in a fire until it became hard.

Smoking was an important part of the annual ceremonies for men. Oil painting by Theodore Morris, Sarasota, Florida.

While inhaling the smoke, the men had talked of what had happened since the last ceremonies, of good hunts and poor hunts, good deeds and bad deeds. Normally, this conversation would have occurred late in the first day, but this year, there had been too much to do.

The Green Corn Ceremony was the only time of the year when men gathered from all the villages around what in the future would be Miami. Some, like The Man, lived near the other end of the sweet-water stream. Others lived along the salty water to either side of the sweet water. Still others lived near the sheet of sweet water that covered much of the interior, feeding The Man's stream and other streams. They would exchange goods occasionally, with the salty-water people providing fish and shellfish for food and tools and the sweet-water people bringing fruit and deer meat. But only during the Green Corn Ceremony did they have time to sit down and talk of their lives.

This was the time of year when marriages were arranged, because it was forbidden for two young people of the same village to wed. The Man was especially interested this year because his oldest son was becoming a man. In one of the sweet-water villages there was someone who had just become a woman, purging her body of impurities every time the moon died. The Man would lose this son, because a young man went to live in his wife's village, but he would gain allies and trading partners. Because of his loss, The Man would expect a large quantity of deer hides from the young woman's family, and the negotiations would take up whatever spare time he might have from his ceremonial duties.

This also was the time to retell the legend of The Visitors, bearers of tame plants and hard earth. A long time ago, long before anyone alive could remember, The Visitors arrived with marvelous new ideas. They demonstrated how kernels could be put into the earth so that food plants would grow where the people wanted. And they explained how fine earth could be collected, molded with plant fi-

Ceremonies were important for girls coming of age who would soon be betrothed. Oil painting by Theodore Morris, Sarasota, Florida.

bers added to help hold its shape, and cooked with fire until it was hard. This was the way the people made bowls to hold food for carrying or eating, and the hollow tubes the men used to inhale the smoke from burning plants.

Tradition had it that the object The Man wore around his neck—made of a round shell incised with a series of concentric circles—was brought by The Visitors. The Man had heard stories of how at a marvelous place along a great lake people in the future would call Okeechobee a long distance to the north, the leader of The Visitors would be buried in a large mound of earth and that on the side toward the rising sun would be buried many items fashioned of shell or bone, including one of the shell circles.

Thanks to the influence of The Visitors, especially in bringing tame plants that required considerable care, the people of South Florida for the first time met in groups including more than one village. Still, in The Man's world there were no leaders with the sort of power wielded among The Visitors. Burials were much simpler, and the shell object was passed on to the next keeper of the medicine bundle.

The Visitors nevertheless had had a great influence on burial practices. The Man's ancestors had always—at least as far as he knew—set out the bodies of their dead until the flesh fell from the bones; then they buried the bones. The Visitors did the same, but their ceremonies were far more elaborate. At that marvelous place along the great lake, The Visitors would place bones on a great wooden platform over a pond, decorated with images of the animals they held sacred, especially birds. During one of their ceremonies, the sacred fire somehow got out of control. It consumed one end of the platform before weakening the supports so much that the rest of the structure crashed into the pond, carrying with it the bones of at least 150 people.

Stunned by the loss of their most sacred site, The Visitors filled the pond with brown dirt and placed a hut atop the resulting mound. Here, their leaders presided over a new means of burial, placing the deceased in the mound soon after death. The great fire, they felt, had been an omen that the old ways were wrong. The Man's people also adopted this form of burial, albeit with much simpler ceremonies.

During their brief occupation west of Ancient Miami, The Visitors had dug a large circular ditch within which the tame plants were grown and a mound nearly as high as a man and as long as the range of a hunter's spear. Near the west end of the mound's flat summit had been a small hut in which a leader lived during the ceremony of the tame plants. The Man had heard stories of these ceremonies, but by his time the mound had long been abandoned and was overgrown with wild plants.

Another way in which The Man's people followed The Visitors' example was in abandoning fibers as a tempering agent for their pots, in favor of coarse sand grains. They did not, however, adopt

The Visitors' technique of crudely polishing the outside of their bowls before putting them in the fire.

Finally, both groups learned that in South Florida there was no way to produce enough tame plants to replace the fruits the women traditionally gathered. The people of the village nearest the ceremonial grounds tended the tame plants. They would allow the stalks of the plants to return to the earth, clean out the ditch surrounding the circle so the ground inside would not flood, and bring in moist soil from elsewhere because the spirits said they must do so if new tame plants were to grow. With all that, there were just enough kernels to feed the people during the special ceremonies. Unknown to them, The Visitors had made the same adjustments at their home village near the lake.

On the third day of the ceremonies, the dancing had begun. The Man's cousin, because of his knowledge of the steps and the rhythms, had sat on a log inside the ceremonial circle and directed the dancers. He had selected a dance leader, an older man from one of the other villages. The others had lined up beside the dance leader and followed him counterclockwise around the ceremonial circle. The dance leader had sung phrases that the others repeated and kept time with a turtle-shell rattle. The Man's cousin had sat and watched, shouting a command if he felt the leader was departing from the traditional cadence or phrasing.

The fourth day had been a time for eating. The men had sat in their special hut and emptied bowl after bowl of deer meat and fruit as the women brought the bowls and set them outside the hut, to which women were forbidden entry. The men had had reason to gorge themselves, for they would not be allowed to eat again until the sun had risen on the second day following.

The Man might have thought about all of this as he arose, but there was no time. Already the sky was getting gray in the east, and there was much to do. He awakened his oldest son, who one day might take over his duties, then went to the next hut to arouse his younger brother. The three walked to the nearest wet area, north of the grounds, undressed, and bathed. The Man sang a special song to give him the wisdom to interpret the medicine so the people would prosper. Upon emerging from the water, the three donned their deerskin breechcloths.

The Man handed his oldest son a deerskin. The Man and his brother returned to the camp while the son walked out of sight to the east. He was going to where his father had hidden the medicine after the last ceremonies, at a spot known only to the two of them. Meanwhile, The Man was supervising two other cousins as they prepared a black drink from dried plant leaves. It was vital that this drink be prepared properly if it was to purify those who used it.

Soon the son reappeared from the east. The deerskin had been tied in a bundle, inside of which were the smaller bundles containing the curing objects: a piece of deer antler, the tooth of a shark, a rock so smooth that it reflected light, pieces of root, the fang of a rattlesnake, hair from a deer, a panther bone, and, most important, several feathers. The Man carefully unwrapped each object, examined it, and then rewrapped it. The bundle then was tied to a pole just outside the ceremonial circle.

By now, the sun was overhead, and it was time for The Man to become a judge. He sat in the men's hut as those who had violated the people's traditions since the last ceremonies were brought before him. Most offenses were minor, such as failing to take part in the hunt or eating another's share of the food, and The Man prescribed a punishment equally minor, such as sitting perfectly still for hours or eating a bitter root. People almost always wanted to do their duty and would be moved as much by the symbolism of the punishment as by its nature. After all, dispensing punishment was the community's way of showing disapproval, and most people sought the approval of those with whom they had to live, eat, and trade.

The Wild One, who lived in a salty-water village not far from The Man's village, was different. He had killed, not once but twice. Two ceremonies ago, The Man's father had ordered The Wild One whipped with branches for taking the life of a fellow villager with his conch-shell ax. Just before this year's ceremonies, The Wild One had killed again, this time holding another villager beneath the salty water until he had died. What was to be done?

Why have you killed again? The Man asked. I don't know, The Wild One answered, it seems as if bad spirits take control of me, and I cannot resist them. Will you accept my punishment? The Man asked. No, The Wild One replied, I tried that once before, and it did no good. In that case there is only one answer, The Man said. I know, The Wild One said.

The Wild One turned and left. Two men from his village fell in beside him, each carrying a conch-shell ax. The three disappeared into the brush to the west, away from the hiding place of the curing objects. Before long, the two men emerged without The Wild One. It had taken them little time to do their work because there would be no burial. The Wild One had forfeited the right to ceremonies that would appease his spirit, and his body would be left on the ground for the animals. His spirit would never rest but would roam the earth.

The Man felt relieved. He had carried out the most solemn of his duties and had none of the apprehension he had felt briefly upon awakening that morning. After all, he was simply obeying the laws of his people as they had been handed down from leader to leader for more time than he had the words to describe. The other men could have refused to carry out his judgments, but they saw that The Man had acted in the traditional way and all were of one mind.

The rest of the day and all that night were spent dancing. It was also at this time that the boys and men were scratched on the arms with stingray spines until the blood flowed. This purged them of impurities, much as the spirits purge the women each time the moon dies. At day's end, The Man again inspected the curing objects. When not dancing, the men spent the night in a new hut to the east of the circle. At midnight they took the black drink, which drove from their bodies whatever impurities had not been carried away with their blood.

At dawn the women left the dancing ground to prepare the final feast. This time, the centerpiece was the newly harvested kernels from the tame plants inside the drainage circle. There was more deer meat and more fruit. Villagers had spent weeks hunting and gathering for this one occasion. Everyone—man, woman, child—ate until full.

After the meal, The Man again went to the medicine bundle, unwrapped each object, inspected it, and rewrapped it. Then he placed the individual packets in a new deerskin and walked off to the east. When he returned, he was empty-handed and the medicine was safe until the next ceremonies. He would tell his son where he had cached it, but no one else.

This act marked the end of the ceremonies. The Man spent the rest of the day completing negotiations for the marriage of his son. His role as keeper of the bundle, and the qualities that had earned him that role, stood him in good stead in getting his price in deer skins.

At day's end, The Man checked the western sky and saw that a new moon had appeared to replace the one that had died in the east. Clearly the spirits were pleased. He had fulfilled his duties well.

The next morning, The Man and his family returned to their home village near the salty water. Others headed to their home villages. They had honored The Ancestors and their traditions, and everyone, alive or dead, was at peace. Except for The Wild One.

6

The Spanish Butt In (A.D. 1568)

The Man had not slept all night, but he was not weary. He and the other Tequesta Indians had spent the night seeking the support of the spirits so they would be successful in killing The Visitors.

The Tequesta, as The Visitors called them, had endured The Visitors since long before The Man was alive, mostly because The Visitors had powerful throwing sticks that made a loud roar accompanied by a flash of light and hurled a hard ball that tore through Tequesta flesh. These sticks could kill from far beyond the range of the Tequesta weapons.

For years, The Visitors had been a tolerable nuisance. From time to time, one of their sailing boats would cast anchor by a big offshore island to which others of their kind had given the name Key Biscayne. Several of The Visitors would cross the bay that had been given the same name in a smaller boat powered by oars and bearing large wooden containers. They would fill these containers with water from what would become known as the Miami River and then immediately depart.

In the old days, The Man had heard, Tequesta men would disappear about the time of a visit. On at least one occasion, according to a story passed down through the generations, The Visitors were seen dragging a struggling Tequesta toward the water boat. When the Tequesta leader was taken by The Visitors to the city they called Havana, he learned that the missing Tequesta had wound up on an island called Hispaniola looking for the yellow rocks from which The Visitors made shiny ornaments.

Then The Visitors decided to move in. The first immigrants were 20 mutineers from a settlement far to the north who had come ashore to get water and were stranded when their fellow fugitives left them. The Calusa, a larger society in southwest Florida that had once many years before ruled the Tequesta and still liked to think of the Tequesta as their vassals, demanded the runaways be turned over to them so they could become sacrifices to the Calusa gods. Nothing doing, said the Tequesta. After all, these newcomers were seen as a sort of status symbol. They had none of the deadly throwing sticks, and their presence was a novelty—welcome relief from the daily grind of wresting a living from the land or the sea.

Twelve of the runaways left when another of the sailing ships stopped by. The men on the ship seemed genuinely surprised that the runaways still were alive. Apparently, the people on the ship that had brought the runaways had said the 20 were killed soon after being stranded. Another ship brought a piece of very thin white material covered with strange markings. The runaways who had stayed with the villagers said the markings spoke to them and said they would be forgiven for having rebelled against their leaders if they would learn to speak as the villagers did and tell the villagers about The Visitors' gods.

Life was not easy on the Biscayne Bay of 1568. The Tequesta had no domesticated plants or beasts. Animals, especially those that inhabited the waters, provided most of their diet, and the pursuit kept them on the move. About the only time they could stay put was during the fall, when the fruits they ate were most plentiful, and the winter, when the roots of the coontie plant were swollen with starch. For ages the Tequesta and their ancestors had made a starchy porridge from those roots, which yielded a substance similar to the arrowroot of South America.

The Miami River yielded sunfish, bowfin, and gar. Biscayne Bay gave the Tequesta large quantities of sea catfish, plus snapper, toad-fish, and turtles. The shallow ocean beyond Key Biscayne produced grunt, barracuda, porgy, jack, and grouper. But the big prizes were the sharks and the whales, found both in the bay and in the ocean. They yielded far more meat than any other source, at sea or on land, but the hunt was both difficult and dangerous.

The Tequesta preferred to hunt in the bay, because the animals could not dive deep to escape. Wooden spears at the ready, the Indi-ans would pole their canoes into known shark and whale areas and wait for an animal to swim by. At this point, the technique differed depending on whether the prey was a shark or a whale. With a shark, the hunt leader would drive a spear with a rope attached into its skin. He would hold on tightly until the shark stopped strug-gling, which meant it had drowned, and then the Indians would tow it to shore for butchering.

With a whale, once the canoes had surrounded the animal in shallow water, a hunter would leap aboard the thrashing mammal and drive a spear into the blowhole, cutting off the animal's air. He would tie a rope to the spear, and the other fishermen would tow the dead whale to the beach, where it would be cut up for meat. A spe-cial prize was the tympanum bones from the whale's ear, which were extracted and venerated as ceremonial objects because at cer-tain angles they resembled human heads.

The Man recalled one hunt in particular when it fell to him to mount the whale and drive the spear. The animal was a fine prize, perhaps 20 feet in length, but it would not give up without a fight. The Man lost track of time as he held desperately to the heaving animal's back. He had heard stories of how a whale once threw a Tequesta from its back and beat him to death with its tail. He also

65

knew an enraged whale could overturn a canoe, and he tried as best he could to steer the animal away from the other hunters by pulling on the spear.

Finally, after what had seemed an eternity but was probably no more than 30 minutes, the animal's air was exhausted and it stopped heaving. The Man then secured the rope tossed to him from the canoe and rode the whale to shore. The feast that followed was the finest in memory, and The Man's bravery and skill that day cemented his position as the hunt leader. In many ways, this was a more prestigious position than village leader. For only during the hunt did a leader have the power to compel obedience with his commands, whereas the village leader could act only with consensus of the other men.

Similar hunting tactics were used for the sea turtles, another good source of meat. Fish would be caught with hook and line or snared with nets woven from plant fibers.

Ashore, the best sources of food were deer and gopher tortoises. The best time to take deer was in the fall, especially if there had been an unusually wet summer and the animals were forced to huddle on the tree islands that dotted the great watery interior. Gopher tortoises were best taken in late spring, when they would frequently emerge from their burrows in the dry scrubland that would be occupied 400 years later by the University of Miami. In either case, overnight trips were required in those pre-Metrorail days. The deer—and the shark, for that matter—had the added bonus of supplying the raw material for tools.

Spring also was the best time to visit a mound surrounded by mangroves on the east side of the bay, alongside a creek that ran into the bay. Huge numbers of fish would rush into the creek as the tide rose and rush back out as it fell. By placing barriers in the creek, using techniques first learned 2,000 years earlier, the villagers would catch large quantities of fish, eating their fill and then drying the rest to carry back to their village.

A Tequesta woman with her child and ceramic bowl.
Oil painting by Theodore Morris, Sarasota, Florida.

Summer trips would take villagers to Key Biscayne and other islands to the south. The women would gather nuts and berries while the men hunted in the sea. The prize catch was the monk seal—150 pounds of meat and bones; it was as valuable as a whale or shark and easier to catch to boot. Beached seals would allow the hunters to approach and would make no attempt at either fight or flight until it was too late.

Whenever the men were hunting and fishing, the women kept busy gathering a variety of foodstuffs. The pinelands north and west of the village produced the coontie root, which was the Tequestas' only plant staple. The Tequesta had refined somewhat the preparation technique practiced at the fishing site 2,000 years previously, grating the roots on a pine board into which shark teeth or small pieces of conch shell had been embedded. From there, the procedure was unchanged: the root would be soaked, the starch extracted and set out to dry.

The pinelands also were the source of saw palmetto berries, while the coastal hammock in which the village was located provided seeds or fruit from the cocoplum, sea grape, mastic, cabbage palm, hog plum, pigeon plum, and oak. The Visitors had brought citrus fruit from Spain but had not introduced it into South Florida.

Deer bones were extremely important to the Tequesta. They were fashioned into points for arrows and harpoons, as well as fishhooks, awls, and ornaments to decorate their bodies. One of the few things of any value the Tequesta had learned from The Visitors was that deer bone could be made into buttons to hold clothing in place. Shark and fish teeth made good cutting tools and drills. They also served as spear or arrow points, as did worked alligator bone and ray spines.

In a land with no hard rocks, shark teeth were the hardest material available locally, another reason the Tequesta would endure the dangers of shark fishing. Once in a long while, they would be able to trade shark teeth for objects made of hard rock from far away, such as two basalt ax heads that were highly valued.

One of The Man's most prized possessions was a pendant made of hard rock. This object told strangers of his status within his village. He wore it on all special occasions and stored it carefully within his hut at other times. When he died, it would be buried with him.

The most important utilitarian uses of wood were for thatch-roof shelters and dugout canoes. People elsewhere used fire to hollow the log for a canoe, but The Man's group did not know of this technique and cut out the wood with axes made of conch shell hafted on wood.

Conch and whelks were not as great a source of food as might be suggested by the size of the giant shell mound at the village in which the Tequesta placed the bodies of their dead leaders—after all, the shells had been deposited for centuries—but the shells themselves were tremendously useful. The lip of a conch shell could be broken off with an antler and ground into a cutting tool or a hammer. (Shark skin was the best grinding tool when available.) The rest of the shell then could be used as a dipper. The central column of a *Busycon* could be broken out and used as a chisel or a pounder. Often, however, the entire shell was used for hammering, either by punching holes in it to admit a pine handle or simply by grasping it and pounding. Smaller shell pieces would be utilized for net weights or ornaments.

Stone could fulfill many of these needs, but there is no hard stone in South Florida; most of the stone used by the Tequesta had been obtained through trades with groups farther north. The Tequesta hoarded any respectably large piece of chert. They would strike it with a deer antler to remove flakes, then trim those flakes by pressing the antler against them until they had crude but serviceable arrow points.

Making these various tools would take up many of the hours when the men were neither hunting nor fishing. Shelter was constructed from pine logs with a roof and walls of palmetto-frond thatch. When not gathering fruit, nuts, or coontie root, the women wove fronds and grasses into mats for sleeping and breechcloths (which comprised the entire wardrobe of males and females), in addition to making fishing nets.

Pottery was made from the best earth available, which wasn't very good. Oil painting by Theodore Morris, Sarasota, Florida.

The women also fashioned open bowls from the sparse local clays, flattening the rims downward with their hands and then adding either pie-crust indentations with their fingers or parallel lines with the tip of a deer antler. The bowls were baked in wood-covered pits until they became hard enough to hold fluids—at least for a little while. Trade brought the Tequesta bowls with a chalky rather than gritty feel and decorated with a checkered pattern.

One story, passed down from generation to generation among the women, concerned excellent bowls made at a site some miles to the north (to be known centuries later as Arch Creek in northern Miami-Dade County) where the fine earth was of especially good quality. But there was not that much of the fine earth, and the last of it had been used up many years ago. By the time of The Visitors' arrival, those wares were only a memory kept alive by word of mouth.

There also were tasks not related directly to food, clothing, or shelter. Wood from pine trees was carved into masks—worn in the dances the Tequesta held during ceremonies to propitiate the spirits that controlled their world—as well as clubs and curved spears carried as symbols of power. At such ceremonies, the Tequesta wore pins carved of deer bones, some of them highly ornamented, keeping time by shaking rattles made of box-turtle shells. Beads to adorn the body were made from shark vertebrae, conch shells, or bird bones.

Many of the ceremonies were held at a special place on the opposite side of the river from their village. The Tequesta knew it as the house of the spirits; people in the twenty-first century would call it the Miami Circle. Ancestors of the Tequesta had built the structure many years ago, and it had been maintained ever since. Nearly every year, one or more of the columns that supported the thatch roof, or the roof itself, had to be replaced.

The villagers undertook this task without complaint, for this was the people's most important building. For a long time (possibly 2,000 years), the house of the spirits had been the spiritual center of the community. Here, the people would appeal to the spirits they believed resided in every animal, every plant, and every object. Here, they held ceremonies for their dead and prepared the bodies

A man fashions a wooden mask for use in ceremonies.
Oil painting by Theodore Morris, Sarasota, Florida.

for burial. After the flesh was removed, the bones would be buried in a mound several hundred paces to the south, accompanied by objects important to the person in life, such as the shell ax heads used to form the dugout canoes.

If the deceased had been a prominent member of the group, the long bones would be placed in a box in the house of the spirits, where the people could pay homage to them, and the other bones would be buried. Aside from this special case, all bodies were treated the same. The sort of hierarchy under which The Visitors lived was unknown to the villagers.

Many years earlier, leaders had been buried beneath the mound at the village, and then beneath the mound to the south, but the Tequesta knew nothing of this.

A very special time came at the start of summer, when the Tequesta journeyed inland to a village on the edge of the great watery interior. In this village, the inhabitants kept alive ceremonies and traditions extending back in time over many years (as far as the Tequesta knew; we now believe it was possibly a millennium). The Tequesta kept track of sunrises from the house of the spirits, and when the sun reached its farthest point north, they would watch until the moon disappeared into the dawn sky. Then they knew it was time to renew their traditions.

Once they arrived at the inland village, the ceremonies would be much as they had been for years and years. The men would fast. The leader of the inland village would bring out the medicine bundle. Offenses would be judged and punishments determined. The bundle would be returned to its hiding place. The men would purge themselves with the black drink. Then everyone would eat as much as possible at the grand feast, the one featuring the new corn.

The Man's life was a busy one. In addition to determining when ceremonies would be held and then directing those ceremonies, he would guide hunters both at sea and on land. Tradition had it that the spirits would determine that a man was destined to be a leader

73

when he entered this world as the oldest son of a leader. On some occasions, however, the spirits would withdraw their approval, and the men of the village would demand that someone else who had demonstrated his skills in the hunt and at the ceremonial grounds be made leader. The Man, however, had led well for several cycles of wet and dry seasons, and the people were happy.

Life changed dramatically in March of 1567 when more Visitors arrived. Thirty warriors armed with firesticks and a priest (actually, a friar, or perhaps a lay brother, but the distinction meant nothing to the Tequesta) had been sent to join the eight remaining runaways. Amid the Tequesta homes the newcomers built their own huts, into which they would take care to go before removing their clothes, because they seemed to be ashamed of their bodies. They placed a palisade of palmetto logs around the entire complex for reasons the Tequesta could not fathom.

The Visitors had said they would bring much food from Havana in their boats, but they brought very little. Instead, they shared the Tequesta stores, which were barely ample in the best of times. Even worse, The Visitors would not allow the Tequesta to go inland for their sacred ceremonies, and the Tequesta felt that without purification they were in great peril both as individuals and as a culture. When serious hunger was setting in during the summer of 1567, most of the Tequesta headed to Key Biscayne, leaving 30 of their number with the 30 alien warriors.

Their mere presence was not the only way in which The Visitors interfered with Tequesta religion. The Tequesta had no problem accepting The Visitors' god, placing him alongside the various gods they worshiped, but The Visitors demanded that the Tequesta abandon their gods and worship just the one. Why should the Tequesta turn away from gods who had seen them through hard times and enabled them to survive and flourish, just on the say-so of some strangers who couldn't even furnish their own food?

Two faiths collided on Biscayne Bay in 1567, with bloody results. Art by Merald Clark, courtesy of Institute of Archaeology and Paleoenvironmental Studies, University of Florida.

And of what use was The Visitors' god? An old Tequesta woman who had taken ill went to the priest, and though he called on his god, she died. A sickly baby girl was brought to the priest shortly afterward, and again he called on his god and again nothing happened. The Tequesta conducted their own ceremonies, but it was too late to save her. Perhaps the Tequesta gods were angered that a foreign god had been consulted.

The language barrier did not make things any easier. The Visitors had some familiarity with the tongues spoken by aborigines of the Caribbean islands, but the Tequesta language, which would defy classification centuries later, was a mystery to their ears.

In January of 1568 Pedro Menéndez de Avilés, the Visitor who had set up a town called St. Augustine far to the north in 1565, had written to one of his people's chief priests that "everywhere the Indians abandoned their idols," a statement the Tequesta would have disputed had they been able to read it. The Tequesta friar, Francisco Villareal, seemed a bit more realistic. He recognized that Tequesta who were ill might be coming to him "out of fear, or with a lack of comprehension, or out of some love or desire for food."

By March of 1568, another rainy season was near, and The Visitors showed no sign of leaving. One of the older Tequesta men could hold back his anger no longer. He told off one of The Visitors in the strongest terms. The Visitor's response was to kill him. That night, the Tequesta resolved that The Visitors would die. They would have resolved to kill the friar as well, but he had left shortly before so that was not an issue.

It was the Tequesta leader who had suggested they avenge the death. Consensus on a course of action had been almost immediate. In light of all the indignities visited upon the villagers by these no-longer-welcome strangers, the people had needed little persuading.

As soon as the sun set, the Tequesta men crossed the river in their canoes and headed for the temple, to seek reassurance among the sacred objects inside. In addition to the whale tympana and the long bones of the dead, the temple held the two basalt axes. The latter had been obtained from far to the north, in an area later people would call the Macon Plateau of Georgia. These various objects had great power to persuade the gods to aid the people in their time of need.

The villagers took with them a shark as long as five human feet that one of their men had speared that day. The Leader interpreted this as a good omen and ordered the shark buried in the temple, with its head facing west. This was no small matter, putting in the earth an animal whose meat could have provided a good meal for the entire village. But in this case, spiritual sustenance was more important.

The Leader had surreptitiously obtained a quantity of the black-drink leaves from the inland village, and he set to work brewing the beverage. Once the men had purged themselves, they spent the rest of the night calling upon their gods to deliver them from their oppressors and asking forgiveness for their failure to purify themselves the previous summer.

The Leader had told them that if the rising sun could be seen from the center of the temple through the door on the east side, it would be a sign the gods were with the Tequesta. As it was the season of the spring equinox, when the sun rises due east, the first rays of light told the Tequesta the day of deliverance was at hand.

They recrossed the river and moved silently into the compound. Evidently neither the sound of their all-night ceremonies nor the silence that descended at dawn alerted their targets. Presumably The Visitors were so used to hearing Tequesta ceremonies, and so ignorant of Tequesta culture, that they had no idea what was afoot.

When they roused for the day, they quickly found out. The Tequesta were upon them in an instant, swinging hatchets made of shell blades hafted to wooden handles. Four of The Visitors fell, to be battered lifeless, and the others fled into the building that had been used by the friar.

The Tequesta dared not follow, for some of The Visitors had had time to get their fire sticks. They could have easily shot down any Tequesta who tried to storm their refuge. But there was no need for the Tequesta to take such a risk. The Visitors had little food or water, and at some point they would have to emerge. The Tequesta had time on their side.

Or did they? Voices from seaward captured their attention. A water boat was approaching, filled with armed warriors. It was not a chance visit; Pedro Menéndez Marquez, nephew of Menéndez de Avilés, had stopped to deliver supplies to the garrison.

The Tequesta knew better than to let themselves be trapped between two bands of Visitors, each with fire sticks. They slipped through the opening in the palisade quickly and hid in the palmetto scrub as the newcomers approached. Their best hope was that the newcomers would be too concerned with the fate of the garrison to pursue them.

They were right. The Menéndez Marquez party quickly transported the survivors and the bodies from the village, a task that required several trips to ferry everyone to the larger boat anchored out of sight beyond Key Biscayne. Before nightfall, they were gone.

The Tequesta reentered the palisade once they were sure no Visitors remained. The Visitors had been careful to take all their fire sticks, as well as the thin white sheets with marks on them that seemed so important to the Spanish priests yet were of no interest and no use to the Tequesta. But in their haste, The Visitors had left many other items behind that would be valuable, especially the large clay storage jars and the cooking pots, made of a hard substance unknown in Florida, that gave off a ringing sound when struck.

After taking what they wanted, the Tequesta set fire to The Visitors' huts and their palisade, just in case the strangers might decide to return and use them again. Then the Tequesta repaired to their own homes for their evening meal. After that, there would be more dancing, but this time it would be to celebrate and to thank the gods for ridding them of these meddlesome strangers. It was going to be nice to have the place all to themselves again.

7

Huddled Masses on the Shore
(A.D. 1761)

The Man had few belongings, and the dugout canoe had room for fewer. He selected mainly his fishing gear. Because the islands to the south would provide little food, he would be dependent upon what he could harvest from the sea. At least the water off the islands was shallow and clear, well suited for spearfishing.

The place he was leaving, where the Miami River empties into Biscayne Bay, had been home to his ancestors since long before anyone in the village could remember. Under other conditions, The Man might have been sad to move away, probably never to return. But fear has a way of pushing nostalgia aside.

When the strangers from a far-off place called Spain first appeared on Biscayne Bay two centuries before The Man's time, the Tequesta had held their own. They had driven off the first group of strangers, killing four of them, and later executed two strangers captured by a smaller group of aborigines to the north and given to the Tequesta as a gift.

The Spaniards had done their best to convince the Tequesta of the superiority of Spanish culture, to the point of taking three

A woman sits on the shore, her thoughts far away. Oil painting by Theodore Morris, Sarasota, Florida.

Tequesta to Spain so they could see for themselves. Several cycles of the moon after the battle in which the four Spaniards were killed, one of the three, a brother of the Tequesta leader whom the Spanish called Don Diego, returned with tales of wonder.

He told of magnificent cities with huge stone buildings, of wondrous clothing decorated with glistening gold and silver, of people in numbers beyond his comprehension who all seemed fascinated with him and his companions. In one huge stone building, evidently a temple to the Spanish god, Don Diego participated in a ceremony during which he agreed to worship the Spanish god in addition to the Tequesta gods. This led to some dispute because the Spanish kept insisting he abandon the Tequesta gods and he kept refusing to do so.

Don Diego's tales so impressed the Tequesta in general and his brother the leader in particular that the Tequesta built a new chapel and asked the Spanish to come back. Early in December 1568, another Jesuit priest, Father Antonio Sedeño, and several companions arrived to set up a new mission. The Tequesta promised to provide the necessary wood for the buildings and a new stockade.

Once again, the Spaniards soon wore out their welcome. The Tequesta insisted on retaining their gods and resisted the newcomers' efforts to make them abandon the old ways, ways that had seen them through more years than they could imagine. If truth be told, the Tequesta still were more interested in Spanish food than in the Spanish god, and their newfound friendliness was in large part concern about alienating people who could make the magnificent things Don Diego had seen. But a people can sacrifice only so much in order to maintain an alliance, and the newcomers asked too much.

After just one cycle of the sun's travels north and south, the Spanish left again. To make sure they stayed away, the Tequesta would either kill or enslave shipwreck victims. In one coup of which the Tequesta were especially proud, they lured a ship's crew of nine to their village with promises of friendship to put them off guard. After an evening of feasting, when the nine were satiated and groggy, the Tequesta fell upon them and killed all but one. The lone survivor was later ransomed back to the Spanish.

The Tequesta maintained their traditional ceremonies. Each spring they went inland to celebrate the harvest of the tame plants. They watched the sun move north and south from their temple on the south side of the river. They fished, and they hunted, and they gathered.

For nearly two centuries, the Spanish made no further attempts to settle. They contented themselves with fishing and trading expeditions. Fishermen would make camp on offshore islands for most of the year (from late August to late March, as the strangers reckoned the yearly cycle) to exploit the rich fishing grounds that had sustained the aborigines for a very long time. The fish would be dried or salted at the island bases. The Spaniards also would take the oil from the livers of sharks and smoke the eggs of mullet and drum; both products were highly valued by the people of Havana.

Other sea products, notably ambergris and the fat of sea otters and manatees, were obtained by the Tequesta and traded to the Spanish, along with hides, fruit, and mats of bark and grass. Especially prized items were live cardinal birds, which the Tequesta would sell to Spanish sailors. The Tequesta were puzzled by the Spaniards' tastes but grateful for the items they received in return: metal tools and ornaments, glass beads and pottery storage jars far larger and of much better quality than anything the Tequesta could produce on their own. Sometimes the Tequesta would take their trade items to Havana in their canoes, but more often they would make their deals with the crews of passing Spanish ships.

Some of the trading had to be done in secret. The Spanish leaders told their people not to provide weapons or rum to the Tequesta, but there always were fishermen willing to ignore those orders. In prac-

A man prepared for battle was a common sight in the eighteenth century. Oil painting by Theodore Morris, Sarasota, Florida.

tice, the Tequesta wound up mostly with hangovers, as they would trade the arms back to the Spanish for more rum.

About 1700, a new group of strangers, aborigines who had been living far to the north, showed up. They were interested in plunder, not trade. They would attack villages of the Tequesta and other South Florida groups, killing many and carrying the rest away. The Tequesta had no way of knowing that the fighting was all part of a struggle between two faraway peoples, the Spanish who claimed Florida and the English who wanted the Spanish out. The invaders, encouraged by the English, started out by destroying the Spanish missions of North Florida and immediately began marauding farther south.

What The Man did know was that his way of life had been utterly disrupted. Life was not that easy in the best of times, and the raiders—not to mention the forlorn refugees driven south by the raiders—had made a normal existence all but impossible. The social structures, which had sustained groups for many years, broke down. Leaders no longer commanded respect. Men beat their women and ignored their children. In many cases, this behavior was due to the influence of the rum, which had become for many a crutch to get through the days.

The raids had strengthened the Tequestas' uneasy alliance with the Spanish. It was not that the aborigines had come to like the Spanish, only that they needed them now for protection as well as for trade goods.

Leadership of the Biscayne Bay band had fallen to The Man upon the death of his father in the year the Spanish called 1755. This had nothing to do with tradition, but rather with The Man's demonstrated skills as both a provider and a mediator. The latter skill was especially important when remnants of societies from all over South Florida, with different histories and different customs, found themselves thrown together. Add to that the psychological damage

Bird effigy tablet from Key Marco, southwest Florida.

to the displaced people, aggravated by the rum, and his task was indeed difficult.

Fortunately, he was up to the challenge. He managed to maintain a semblance of organization. He personally led the trading initiatives, bargaining firmly with the Spanish to get his people the best deal. Many years earlier (107 years, to be precise, though the Tequesta had no concept of numbers that large), the Spanish had paid for a great quantity of ambergris with broken metal implements that were of no more use to the Tequesta than they had been to the Spanish. The Man was determined that his people would never again be cheated in that way.

He also played a pivotal role in spiritual matters, reconciling the bird worship of other societies in South Florida with the Tequestas' veneration of fish. He appointed two men from other groups to assist him. One communicated with the spirits through trances, whereas the other was both a seer—of events far away in both space and time—and a healer.

But these tasks left too little time for more traditional activities. The Man often could not find the hours to lead his people to the bounty of the waters, whether by cruising the bay flats in his dugout in search of fish to spear or by exploring deeper waters offshore for schools of fish to net. He was too busy to fashion spears from lengths of pine tipped with stingray spines that had to be de-barbed and sharpened, a time-consuming operation. Nor did he have time to maintain the simple shelter, similar to a Seminole chickee, in which he and his family lived.

Fear of the raiders made him apprehensive every time The Woman went out to collect berries or palm fronds or coontie root. Fortunately, she no longer had to search for the poor-quality sandy clay from which the Tequesta once had fashioned crude open pots. The pots the Indians obtained from the Spanish were far better. They would hold liquids without seeping, because the Spanish had much hotter fires in which to make them. Still, she did have to go after food, and the woods were often dangerous.

The first raids had occurred in 1704, years before The Man was born. The invaders from the north had burned villages, killing some of the South Floridians and chasing others into hiding. Most, however, were captured and taken far away to the north, to an English city called Charleston, where they were sold into slavery.

The Man's grandfather was one of the 270 South Floridians brought to Havana by the Spanish in March of 1711. Another 1,700 Indians would have gladly joined the lucky 270 in Havana, but the ships did not have enough room for them. Several Indian leaders previously brought to Havana for negotiations had told the Spanish that all the natives "were of a mind to be converted to our holy Catholic faith," but in fact the Indians had no interest in the Spanish god. The South Floridians were seeking to save their bodies, not their souls. In fact, the South Floridians had ceased to believe in a soul that survives after death because their supplications for relief from the raiders had apparently fallen on deaf ears.

The migration turned out badly all around. More than 200 of the South Floridians soon died of maladies against which neither medicine nor prayer, aboriginal or Spanish, could prevail. The social structure of the survivors, based on kinship groups in which a child belonged to the group of the mother, was shattered. Some of these survivors moved in with Spanish families. Another 16 or 18, including The Man's grandfather, elected to return to Florida when they learned the Spanish would not bring any more of their kinsmen to Havana.

By this time, any illusions the Spanish might have had about the South Floridians' motives had been shattered. The Indians, "being inclined by their nature to negotiate in bad faith, any whatsoever kindly actions that are expended on them are wasted," the governor of Cuba wrote in a letter to the king of Spain in July of 1732. "There has been no lack of examples of ones who, after having been brought up here and after having spent 30 years in the Christian school, have returned to [Florida] to follow their evil nature." The only way to convert the South Floridians was at gunpoint, he wrote.

He undoubtedly was soured by the failure of an effort earlier that year to entice more Indians to Havana. Fourteen leaders had been brought to Havana and, along with a few of the remaining émigrés from the 1711 migration, had accompanied Spanish negotiators back to Florida. For three days, the Florida Indians had eaten the Spaniards' food and drunk their wine. On the fourth day, the Indians had disappeared into the wilderness, taking their dismantled huts with them. The Spanish had waited three more days, then returned to Havana.

The last attempt by the Spanish to provide any "help" to their South Florida "subjects" occurred in July of 1743, when two Jesuit priests made a brief visit to the Miami River village. The Man's father and two other Indian leaders had asked the Spanish "[to] provide us with missionaries at once that they may go to our lands to teach us the holy Catholic faith," according to a document purported to be in their words. In fact, the Indians continued to be more interested in Spanish food than in the Spanish god, and the Spanish knew this. Also, the Spanish preferred to bring Indians to Cuba for instruction, so they could better control the Indians' movements. But the Spanish were aware of how badly that had worked out in the past. Not only had the Indians fared poorly in Havana, but their presence made some Spanish settlers uncomfortable. So the two priests, Fathers Joseph María Monaco and Joseph Javier Alaña, were sent from Havana.

They found 180 people who constituted all that was left of the Tequesta, the Ais and Jaega Indians of the East Coast, the Calusa Indians of southwest Florida, and the Keys Indians. The village had only five huts, and the people had to abandon them for much of the year to seek food elsewhere. Frequently, they would hitch rides to the more distant islands with Spanish fishermen, whose craft were larger and better appointed than the aboriginal dugouts.

The Man, who was only a boy at the time, remembered that his father and the other elders quickly fell to arguing with the visitors. The Indian leaders agreed to accept the Spanish god only on the condition they be allowed to keep their own gods as well. Moreover, the Spanish would have to feed and clothe the South Floridians and promise not to punish their children while teaching them the Spanish religion.

The Spanish demanded that the Indians stop sacrificing children at the funerals of their leaders. That was one request the Indians could honor easily, as human sacrifice had not been practiced for generations, a fact of which the Spanish evidently were ignorant.

The Spanish did little to endear themselves to their hosts. With an armed ship hovering offshore to intimidate the villagers, The Visitors destroyed both the village church and the image of a bird that figured in the villagers' burial rituals. The Spanish also would have destroyed the fish image that was the villagers' principal ceremonial object, but the villagers hid it first.

In another attempt to subdue the villagers, "Fr. Alaña, with cunning and cajolery, had brought to Havana the leading Indians who could stir up trouble in the village." Fortunately for the villagers, the priest did not realize that The Man's father was one of their leaders, and he was left in Florida to stir as best as he could.

The Spanish were quick to criticize the villagers' drunkenness but reluctant to lay any blame on the Spanish fishermen who sold liquor to the villagers. The priests were especially irritated that the villagers countered Spanish criticisms by pointing out that The Visitors used wine in their religious services. The Spanish also criticized the villagers for engaging in constant warfare that was thinning their ranks without noting that the villagers were not the aggressors.

In addition to not being clear on the leadership, the Spanish understood little of the villagers' beliefs. The villagers were concerned that the spirits pervading everything around them would be displeased if the living did not honor the dead with the proper ceremonies, but they had no terror of the dead, as Spanish writers claimed. Also, one of the villagers was known as The Wise One for his ability to summon good spirits and banish evil spirits. But the villagers did not consider him to be either a bishop or a god, as the Spanish claimed they did.

In his report, Father Alaña condemned the Indians' "errors, idolatries and superstitions" and reserved special contempt for "the very tenacious attachment with which they maintain all this and the ridicule they direct toward beliefs contrary to theirs." The villagers felt the same way about the Spanish religion, though they did not have the means to preserve their views on paper. The villagers saw no distinction between the objects they worshiped and the images the Spanish used in their ceremonies.

The priests ordered a stockade built and garrisoned with a dozen soldiers. They recommended that a settlement be established complete with armed soldiers to keep the villagers from fleeing into the countryside. "With the measures proposed, or those that your excellency may find more appropriate," Father Alaña wrote in his report to the governor of Cuba, "their idolatry will be abolished and the true religion will be established among this people." Fortunately for the villagers, Spanish authorities in Havana decided instead to abandon the stockade.

The villagers got a measure of revenge, at least against the English, five years later when a ship foundered near Key Biscayne with 12 on board. Sixty villagers descended on the wreck in 20 canoes, one of which flew an English flag to make the crew think the visit was a friendly one. The sailors soon learned differently; the villagers seized their firearms and used them to kill 11 of the 12. The survivor, a black man named Briton Hammon, was beaten and taken prisoner. His life was spared only because he clearly was not an Englishman like the others. Hammon was held five weeks, until he was rescued and taken to Havana in a Spanish vessel. The Spanish gave the villagers 10 dollars for their trouble.

That would be the villagers' last hurrah. By 1761, the pressure from the north had become intolerable. The villagers' only chance for survival was to get to an island where the invaders could not easily reach them. And that is why The Man was packing his canoe that morning. Besides the spears, The Man loaded his best fishing net, a cooking pot he had obtained from a Spanish fisherman, and a couple of woven sacks full of berries. When he was done, he called The Woman, who rounded up The Boy and The Girl and brought them to the shore. They settled themselves near the front of the canoe. The Man pushed it away from the shore, jumped into the rear, and began poling through the shallow water.

He did not look back.

Afterword

The Man and his family would never return to Biscayne Bay.

On the islands to which they fled—called Los Mártires (The Martyrs) by the Spanish because their rocks supposedly resembled martyrs, and known today as the Florida Keys—the villagers would earn a reputation for fierceness toward any sailor who fell into their grasp. Bernard Romans, an Englishman who visited Florida in 1770–71, called them "the dread and terror of the seamen. . . . The inhumanity committed . . . on shipwrecked mariners is shocking even to barbarians. . . . The people from [Nassau] who came here for turtle or mahogany wood came always armed and had frequent brushes with [the Indians]."

The strangers from the north, now mostly Creek Indians, were another matter. As Romans put it, "Even here the water did not protect them against the inroads from the Creeks." In 1762, invaders had attacked and overpowered a group of South Florida canoes on a trading trip to Havana.

The next year, the Spanish, having lost Havana to the English in what Europeans called the Seven Years' War, would regain their city only by giving Florida to the English. Whatever reservations they might have had about the Spanish, the villagers had no desire to stay on under the rule of the hated English. As Romans described it, "the remnant of this people, consisting of about 80 families, left this last possession of their native land and went to Havana." The Man, The Woman, The Boy, and The Girl constituted one of those 80 families.

With the villagers gone, the Creek invaders would set themselves up on the peninsula and would become known as Seminoles, apparently from the Spanish word for "runaways." They soon would have their own problems with Europeans, but that's another story. For the Ancient Miamians, life in South Florida had ended.

Bibliographic Essay

CHAPTER 2. THE ICE AGE IN A DRY LAND (8000 B.C.)

Archaeological information on paleoindians from South Florida is very slim, limited essentially to the investigations by Robert S. Carr: "Preliminary Report on Archaeological Excavations at the Cutler Fossil Site in Southern Florida" (1986); "Preliminary Report on Excavations at the Cutler Fossil Site (8Da2001) in Southern Florida" (1986). It is from these investigations that the description of the site and the list of animal bones and other artifacts are taken. Descriptions of paleoindian tools come from Barbara A. Purdy's *Florida's Prehistoric Stone Technology* (1981). The existence of wooden spears is assumed from the design of the points; that of spear-throwers, from the report of spear sockets at Warm Mineral Springs by W. A. Cockrell and Larry Murphy, "Pleistocene Man in Florida" (1978). A boomerang and an oaken mortar were found at Little Salt Spring: see C. J. Clausen et al., "Little Salt Spring, Florida: A Unique Underwater Site" (1979).

Behavior, of humans and animals alike, is assumed by analogy to the present day. Major sources of ideas for behavior of the hunters are Elman R. Service's description of the Arunta of Australia in *Profiles in Ethnology* (1971) and the summary of paleoindian hunting by Robert F. Spencer et al. in *The Native Americans* (1965). Burial practices are suggested by the findings of John Beriault and his co-authors in "The Archaeological Salvage of the Bay West Site, Collier County, Florida" (1981). Peccary behavior comes from Hans Frädrich's description of the collared peccary in *Grzimek's Animal Life Encyclopedia* (1975). The racial affinity of paleoindians is assumed from work summarized by Sharon Begley and Andrew Murr in "The First Americans" (1999). The environmental description is based on Victor A. Carbone's "Late Quaternary Environments in Florida and the Southeast" (1983).

The fullest account of our knowledge of paleoindians in Florida is in Jerald T. Milanich's *Archaeology of Precolumbian Florida* (1994), while the best description for South Florida is in my *Prehistoric Peoples of South Florida* (1993). An excellent report on a Florida paleoindian site (near Tampa) is *Harney Flats: A Florida Paleo-Indian Site* (1987) by I. Randolph Daniel Jr. and Michael Wisenbaker.

CHAPTER 3. SEIZING THE OPPORTUNITIES (2000 B.C.)

Much of this chapter must be conjecture owing to the paucity of physical evidence from Archaic sites in Miami-Dade County. We are, however, reasonably sure of burial practices due to discoveries at several sites, notably the Cheetum tree-island site that is used in this reconstruction. Cheetum data come from two unpublished reports: Christine Newman, "Preliminary Report of Archaeological Investigations Conducted at the Cheetum Site, Dade County, Florida" (1986) and Joseph H. Davis Jr. et al., "Investigation of Human Remains from the Cheetum Site (8Da-1058)" (1985). Other Archaic cemeteries are discussed in reports by Robert S. Carr, "Salvage Excavations at Two Prehistoric Cemeteries in Dade County, Florida" (1981), and Carr, M. Yasar Iscan, and Richard A. Johnson, "A Late Archaic Cemetery in South Florida" (1984). The second tree island is Bamboo Mound, reported by Gary N. Beiter, "Salvage and Excavation of Bamboo Mound (8DA94), Dade County, Florida: A Multi-Component Site" (2001).

Techniques for obtaining food are taken in large part from Lewis H. Larson's *Aboriginal Subsistence Technology on the Southeastern Coastal Plain during the Late Prehistoric Period* (1980). Information on the nature of tree hammocks comes from F. C. Craighead Sr., "Hammocks of South Florida" (1974), and the rising sea level is discussed by Rhodes W. Fairbridge in "The Holocene Sea-Level Record in South Florida" (1974). The role of deer and bear in Archaic society is assumed from the work of James Mooney, *Myths of the Cherokee and Sacred Formulas of the Cherokees* (1982). The chronology for the Archaic period is mine.

CHAPTER 4. HARVESTING THE BOUNTY OF THE SEA (500 B.C.)

The site of the village is the now-destroyed Surfside mounds, which were on Bay Drive between 91st and 94th streets. Major reports on the mounds, the vegetation, and the objects found within the mounds are those by John Kunkel Small, *From Eden to Sahara: Florida's Tragedy* (1929), and Gordon R. Willey, *Excavations in Southeast Florida* (1949). Much information on food-gathering techniques comes from Lewis H. Larson's *Aboriginal Subsistence Technology on the Southeastern Coastal Plain during the Late Prehistoric Period* (1980). Robin C. Brown provided some food-gathering information, as well as a description of aboriginal shelter in *Florida's First People* (1994) . The assumption of a 2,500-year-old occupation comes from Rhodes W. Fairbridge; by his chronology in "The Holocene Sea-Level Record in South Florida" (1974), this is roughly when the base of both the village deposits and the burial mound would have been three to four feet above sea level. According to John M. Goggin, "The Archeology of the Glades Area, Southern Florida" (n.d.), the base was three to four feet below sea level in 1933.

The canal is mentioned in a report by Karl Squires, "Pre-Columbian Man in Southern Florida" (1941).

CHAPTER 5. TAME PLANTS AND HARD EARTH (A.D. 500)

By far the most important source for this chapter is Louis Capron's description of the Green Corn Dance in "The Medicine Bundles of the Florida Seminole and the Green Corn Dance" (1953). Other information comes from Charles Hudson's *The Southeastern Indians* (1976). The assumption of corn cultivation within a drainage circle is based on analogy with uses postulated by William H. Sears in *Fort Center: An Archaeological Site in the Lake Okeechobee Basin* (1982). He also is the source for the idea that the Green Corn Dance was practiced as many as 1,500 years ago. Admittedly, most archaeologists do not share these views.

The presence of ceramic platform pipes resembling objects from Midwestern Hopewell is assumed on the basis of George M. Luer's analysis of objects from the Ortona site in Glades County, "Pipe Fragments from Ortona, South Florida: Comments on Platform Pipe Styles, Functions and Middle Woodland Exchange" (1995).

The circle near the Green Corn Dance site is the Dade Circle reported by Robert S. Carr in "Prehistoric Circular Earthworks in South Florida" (1985), and the mound is Miami Sand Mound 3, reported by John M. Goggin in "The Archeology of the Glades Area, Southern Florida" (n.d.). The assumption of a shift to extended burials is based on analogy to data reported for Fort Center by Sears. The round shell object is assumed to be identical to one reported by Gordon R. Willey for the Belle Glade site in *Excavations in Southeast Florida* (1949).

The idea of a temple on the south shore of the Miami River dating back as many as 1,500 years is based on my visit and conversations with Robert S. Carr regarding the circular trench and holes found in limestone at a construction site atop the Brickell Point site in 1998, as well as published accounts by Carr and John Ricisak, "Preliminary Report on Salvage Archaeological Investigations of the Brickell Point Site (8DA12), Including the Miami Circle" (2000) and Brent R. Weisman, Herschel E. Shepard, and George M. Luer, "The Origin and Significance of the Brickell Point Site (8DA12), Also Known as the Miami Circle" (2000). Some archaeologists, notably Jerald T. Milanich, question whether the carved holes actually are prehistoric.

CHAPTER 6. THE SPANISH BUTT IN (A.D. 1568)

By far the most important single source for this chapter is the undated two-volume report on the Granada site, as part of the Tequesta village is known, prepared for the City of Miami by the Florida Division of Archives, History and Records Management. The volume exploring the archaeological record, *Excavations at the Granada Site*, was written by John W. Griffin and eight other scientists, the one dealing with the historical record, *Where the River Found the Bay: Historical Study of the Granada Site, Miami, Florida* by Arva Moore Parks.

This two-volume report provided the data on the animals and plants used by the Tequesta and the areas in which they were obtained, with the exception of the whale and monk-seal data, which come from Lewis H. Larson, *Aboriginal Subsistence Technology on the Southeastern Coastal Plain during the Late Prehistoric Period* (1980). The Granada report also tells what tools the Tequesta had and of what they were fashioned. Some of the translations of Spanish documents on which I depended are in the Parks volume. Others are in the writings of Jeanette Thurber Connor, *Colonial Records of Spanish Florida* (1925), John H. Hann, *Missions to the Calusa* (1991), and Ruben Vargas Ugarte, "The First Jesuit Mission in Florida" (1935).

The fish-trapping would have occurred at the Surfside site, which by the time of the Tequesta would have been an island surrounded by mangroves, based on the twentieth-century report of John Kunkel Small, *From Eden to Sahara: Florida's Tragedy* (1929).

The function of the rock pendant is based on John F. Reiger's conclusions in "Artistry, Status, and Power: How 'Plummet'-Pendants Probably Functioned" (1999). The wood masks are assumed on the basis on those reported by Marion Spjut Gilliland in *The Material Culture of Key Marco, Florida* (1975). The clubs and curved spear are those reported by John M. Goggin in "A Prehistoric Wooden Club from South Florida" (1942) and Barbara A. Purdy in *The Art and Archaeology of Florida's Wetlands* (1991); the interpretations of their function are mine.

The shark burial is described in an unsigned *Florida Antiquity* article, "Fate of Miami Circle to Be Decided in Court" (1999), and the Carr-Ricisak article indicates it could be of the right age. The idea of placing shell ax heads with burials comes from a report by Carr and John F. Reiger, "Stombus Celt Caches in Southeast Florida" (1980). The Brickell Point site also produced monk-seal teeth and the basalt ax heads, the origin of which was reported by Jacqueline Eaby Dixon et al. in "Provenance of Stone Celts from the Miami Circle Archaeological Site" (2000).

The discussion of burial practices is based on reports by John M. Goggin in "The Archeology of the Glades Area, Southern Florida" (n.d.), Andrew E. Douglass, "Earth and Shell Mounds on the Atlantic Coast of Florida" (1885), and Carr et al., *A Due Diligence Archaeological Assessment of Brickell Park, Miami, Florida* (2001).

It should be noted that Carr and Ricisak believe there was little activity in the area after A.D. 1200. I would argue that the presence of the shark burial shows at least some ceremonial use and that the absence of post-1200 aboriginal ceramics or Spanish ware may indicate simply that those items were not used in ceremonies.

CHAPTER 7. HUDDLED MASSES ON THE SHORE (A.D. 1761)

The most important single source for this account is the translations of Spanish documents provided by John H. Hann in his 1991 book *Missions to the Calusa*. Other material comes from the undated volumes by John W. Griffin et al., *Excavations at the Granada Site*, and Arva Moore Parks, *Where the River Found the Bay: Historical Study of the Granada Site, Miami, Florida* on prehistoric and historic occupation at the mouth of the Miami River and from Jeanette Thurber Connor's 1925 translations of other Spanish documents, *Colonial Records of Spanish Florida*. Spanish fishing activities are described in detail by James W. Covington in "Trade Relations between Southwestern Florida and Cuba—1600–1840."

The importance of fish imagery to the people of Biscayne Bay comes from the Alaña report as translated by John H. Hann. Frank Hamilton Cushing, in *Exploration of Ancient Key Dwellers' Remains on the Gulf Coast of Florida* (1973), and William H. Sears, *Fort Center: An Archaeological Site in the Lake Okeechobee Basin* (1982), report bird images for the southwest coast and the interior. The ordeal of Briton Hammon comes from his 1760 account of the incident, *A Narrative of the Uncommon Sufferings and Surprising Deliverance of Briton Hammon*.

References

Anonymous. "Fate of Miami Circle to Be Decided in Court." *Florida Antiquity* 6, no. 1 (1999): 1–2.

Begley, Sharon, and Andrew Murr. "The First Americans." *Newsweek*, April 26, 1999, 50–57.

Beiter, Gary N. "Salvage and Excavation of Bamboo Mound (8DA94), Dade County, Florida: A Multi-Component Site." *Florida Anthropologist* 54, no. 1 (2001): 30–48.

Beriault, John, Robert Carr, Jerry Stipp, Richard Johnson, and Jack Meeder. "The Archaeological Salvage of the Bay West Site, Collier County, Florida." *Florida Anthropologist* 34, no. 2 (1981): 39–58.

Blank, Joan Gill. *Key Biscayne*. Sarasota, Fla.: Pineapple Press, 1996.

Brown, Robin C. *Florida's First People*. Sarasota, Fla.: Pineapple Press, 1994.

Bullen, Ripley B. *A Guide to the Identification of Florida Projectile Points*. Gainesville, Fla.: Kendall Books, 1975.

Capron, Louis. "The Medicine Bundles of the Florida Seminole and the Green Corn Dance." *Bureau of American Ethnology Bulletin* 151 (1953): 155–210.

Carbone, Victor A. "Late Quaternary Environments in Florida and the Southeast." *Florida Anthropologist* 32, nos. 1–2 (1983): 3–17.

Carr, Robert S. "Salvage Excavations at Two Prehistoric Cemeteries in Dade County, Florida." Paper presented at 45th annual meeting, Florida Academy of Sciences, Winter Park, 1981.

———. "Prehistoric Circular Earthworks in South Florida." *Florida Anthropologist* 38, no. 4 (1985): 288–301.

———. "Preliminary Report on Archaeological Excavations at the Cutler Fossil Site in Southern Florida." Paper presented at 51st annual meeting, Society for American Archeology, New Orleans, 1986.

———. "Preliminary Report on Excavations at the Cutler Fossil Site (8Da2001) in Southern Florida." *Florida Anthropologist* 39, no. 3 (1986): 231–32.

Carr, Robert S., and John F. Reiger. "Stombus Celt Caches in Southeast Florida." *Florida Anthropologist* 33, no. 2 (1980): 66–74.

Carr, Robert S., and John Ricisak. "Preliminary Report on Salvage Archaeological Investigations of the Brickell Point Site (8DA12), Including the Miami Circle." *Florida Anthropologist* 43, no. 4 (2000): 260–84.

Carr, Robert S., M. Yasar Iscan, and Richard A. Johnson. "A Late Archaic Cemetery in South Florida." *Florida Anthropologist* 37, no. 4 (1984): 172–88.

Carr, Robert S., Jeff Ransom, Mark Lance, and Alison Elgart-Berry. *A Due Diligence Archaeological Assessment of Brickell Park, Miami, Florida.* Archaeological and Historical Conservancy Technical Report 312, Miami, 2001.

Clausen, C. J., A. D. Cohen, Cesare Emiliani, J. A. Holman, and J. J. Stipp. "Little Salt Spring, Florida: A Unique Underwater Site." *Science* 203 (1979): 609–14.

Cockrell, W. A., and Larry Murphy. "Pleistocene Man in Florida." *Archaeology of Eastern North America* 6 (1978): 1–13.

Connor, Jeanette Thurber, ed. and trans. *Colonial Records of Spanish Florida.* DeLand: Florida State Historical Society, 1925.

Covington, James W. "Trade Relations between Southwestern Florida and Cuba, 1600–1840." *Florida Historical Quarterly* 38, no. 2 (1959): 114–28.

Craighead, F. C., Sr. "Hammocks of South Florida." In *Environments of South Florida: Present and Past,* edited and compiled by Patrick J. Gleason, 53–60. Miami: Miami Geological Society, 1974.

Cushing, Frank Hamilton. *Exploration of Ancient Key Dwellers' Remains on the Gulf Coast of Florida.* New York: AMS Press, 1973.

Daniel, I. Randolph, Jr., and Michael Wisenbaker. *Harney Flats: A Florida Paleo-Indian Site.* Farmingdale, N.Y.: Baywood Publishing, 1987.

Davis, Joseph H., Jr., Joseph H. Davis, M.D., and Richard R. Souviron, D.D.S. "Investigation of Human Remains from the Cheetum Site (8Da-1058)." Manuscript, 1985.

Davis, T. Frederick. "Juan Ponce de León's Voyages to Florida." *Florida Historical Quarterly* 14, no. 1 (1935): 1–70.

Dixon, Jacqueline Eaby, Kyla Simons, Loretta Leist, Christopher Eck, John Ricisak, John Gifford, and Jeff Ryan. "Provenance of Stone Celts from the Miami Circle Archaeological Site." *Florida Anthropologist* 53, no. 4 (2000): 328–41.

Douglass, Andrew E. "Earth and Shell Mounds on the Atlantic Coast of Florida." *American Antiquarian and Oriental Journal* (March 1885): 140–47.

Fairbridge, Rhodes W. "The Holocene Sea-Level Record in South Florida." In *Environments of South Florida: Present and Past,* edited and compiled by Patrick J. Gleason, 223–32. Miami: Miami Geological Society, 1974.

Frädrich, Hans. "Swine and Peccaries." In *Grzimek's Animal Life Encyclopedia,* edited by Bernhard Grzimek, 104–8. New York: Van Nostrand and Reinhold, 1975.

Gannon, Michael, ed. *The New History of Florida.* Gainesville: University Press of Florida, 1996.

Gilliland, Marion Spjut. *The Material Culture of Key Marco, Florida.* Gainesville: University Presses of Florida, 1975.

Goggin, John M. "The Archeology of the Glades Area, Southern Florida." Manuscript, n.d.

———. "A Prehistoric Wooden Club from South Florida." *American Anthropologist* 44 (1942): 327–28.

———. *Spanish Majolica in the New World.* Yale University Publications in Anthropology 72. New Haven: Yale University Press, 1968.

Griffin, John W., et al. *Excavations at the Granada Site.* Tallahassee: Florida Division of Archives, History and Records Management, n.d.

Hammon, Briton. *A Narrative of the Uncommon Suffering and Surprising Deliverance of Briton Hammon.* Boston: Green and Russell, 1760.

Hann, John H., ed. and trans. *Missions to the Calusa.* Gainesville: University of Florida Press, 1991.

Hudson, Charles. *The Southeastern Indians.* Knoxville: University of Tennessee Press, 1976.

Iscan, Mehmet Yasar, Morton H. Kessel, and Robert S. Carr. "Human Remains from the Archaic Brickell Bluff Site." *Florida Anthropologist* 46, no. 4 (1993): 277–81.

Larson, Lewis H. *Aboriginal Subsistence Technology on the Southeastern Coastal Plain during the Late Prehistoric Period.* Gainesville: University Presses of Florida, 1980.

Luer, George M. "Pipe Fragments from Ortona, South Florida: Comments on Platform Pipe Styles, Functions and Middle Woodland Exchange." *Florida Anthropologist* 48, no. 4 (1995): 301–8.

McGoun, William E. *Prehistoric Peoples of South Florida.* Tuscaloosa: University of Alabama Press, 1993.

Merzer, Martin. "Tequesta on Verge of Vanishing Again." *Miami Herald,* February 14, 1999.

Miami–West India Archaeological Society and Broward County Archaeological Society. "The Arch Creek Site, Dade County." *Florida Anthropologist* 28, no. 1 (1975): 1–13.

Milanich, Jerald T. *Archaeology of Precolumbian Florida.* Gainesville: University Press of Florida, 1994.

Milanich, Jerald T., and Nara B. Milanich. "Revisiting the Freducci Map: A Description of Juan Ponce de León's 1513 Florida Voyage?" *Florida Historical Quarterly* 74, no. 3 (1996): 319–28.

Milanich, Jerald T., and Susan Milbrath, eds. *First Encounters: Spanish Explorations in the Caribbean and the United States, 1492–1570.* Ripley P. Bullen Series. Gainesville: University of Florida Press, 1989.

Mooney, James. *Myths of the Cherokee and Sacred Formulas of the Cherokees.* Nashville, Tenn.: Charles and Randy Elder, Booksellers, 1982.

Newman, Christine. "Preliminary Report of Archaeological Investigations Conducted at the Cheetum Site, Dade County, Florida." Miami: Archaeological and Historical Conservancy, 1986.

Parks, Arva Moore. *Where the River Found the Bay: Historical Study of the Granada Site, Miami, Florida.* Tallahassee: Florida Division of Archives, History and Records Management, n.d.

Purdy, Barbara A. *Florida's Prehistoric Stone Technology: A Study of the Flintworking Technique of Early Florida Stone Implement Makers.* Gainesville: University Presses of Florida, 1981.

———. *The Art and Archaeology of Florida's Wetlands.* Boca Raton: CRC Press, 1991.

Reiger, John F. "Artistry, Status, and Power: How 'Plummet'-Pendants Probably Functioned." *Florida Anthropologist* 52, no. 4 (1999): 227–40.

Sears, William H. "Southeastern United States, 400 B.C.–A.D. 1000." Manuscript, n.d.

———. *Fort Center: An Archaeological Site in the Lake Okeechobee Basin.* Gainesville: University Presses of Florida, 1982.

Service, Elman R. *Profiles in Ethnology.* New York: Harper and Row, 1971.

Small, John Kunkel. *From Eden to Sahara: Florida's Tragedy.* Lancaster, Pa.: Science Press, 1929.

Spencer, Robert F., Jesse D. Jennings, et al. *The Native Americans.* New York: Harper and Row, 1965.

Squires, Karl. "Pre-Columbian Man in Southern Florida." *Tequesta* 1 (1941): 39–46.

Tebeau, Charlton W. *A History of Florida.* Coral Gables: University of Miami Press, 1971.

Thorhaug, Anitra, ed., and Al Volker, coordinating ed. *Biscayne Bay: Past / Present / Future.* Special Report no. 5. University of Miami Sea Grant, 1976.

Vargas Ugarte, Ruben. "The First Jesuit Mission in Florida." *Historical Records and Studies, United States Catholic Conference* 25 (1935): 59–148.

Weisman, Brent R., Herschel E. Shepard, and George M. Luer. "The Origin and Significance of the Brickell Point Site (8DA12), Also Known as the Miami Circle." *Florida Anthropologist* 53, no. 4 (2000): 342–46.

Whitfield, Peter. *The Charting of the Oceans.* Rohnert Park, Calif.: Pomegranate Books, 1996.

Whorisky, Peter. "The Holes, the Eye, the Axes: Mysteries May Go Unsolved." *Miami Herald,* February 14, 1999.

Willey, Gordon R. *Excavations in Southeast Florida.* Yale University Publications in Anthropology 42. New Haven: Yale University Press, 1949.

Index

Ramada Dupont Plaza Hotel, 2, 13–15
Reed, Frank, 6, 8
Romans, Bernard, 92–93
Royal Palm hotel, 14

St. Augustine, 2, 76
Sears, William H., xiii
Sedeño, Father Antonio, 81
Seven Years' War, 92
Small, John Kunkel, xii, 13
Spaniards: enslavement of Indians by, 3,
    63–64; fishing by, on offshore is-
    lands, 82; trade with Tequesta by, 82
—at Tequesta: firearms of, 63; first mis-
    sion of, 74–78; first settlers, 64, 79;

food, 74; killing of, by Tequesta, 77;
    killing of warrior, 76; second mission
    of, 81; taking of three Tequesta to
    Spain, 79, 81; third mission of, 88–
    90; village and palisade, 74; water
    parties, 63; writing, 64
Surfside site, xii, 13, 16

Tebeau, Charlton W., xii
Tequesta, 5

Villareal, Francisco, 76

Whitfield, Peter, 3
Wolf, dire, 20–21

William E. McGoun is a semiretired journalist. His dissertation was published as *Prehistoric Peoples of South Florida* (University of Alabama Press, 1993). He also is the author of three history books and numerous newspaper articles during a 42-year career with newspapers in West Palm Beach, Fort Lauderdale, Miami Beach, and Miami. He is currently a contributing editor at the *Asheville* (N.C.) *Citizen-Times.*